LICENSE TO PARENT

LICENSE TO PARENT

How My Career as
a Spy Helped Me
Raise Resourceful,
Self-Sufficient Kids

CHRISTINA HILLSBERG
with RYAN HILLSBERG

G. P. PUTNAM'S SONS
NEW YORK

PUTNAM
— EST. 1838 —

G. P. PUTNAM'S SONS
Publishers Since 1838
An imprint of Penguin Random House LLC
penguinrandomhouse.com

Hardcover ISBN: 9780593191118
eBook ISBN: 9780593191125

Printed in the United States of America
1st Printing

BOOK DESIGN BY KRISTIN DEL ROSARIO

To Ryan:
My rock, my biggest supporter, and my partner.
This book is a testament to the amazing father you are.
We are the luckiest.

To the Bigs:
This book exists mostly because of you.
Thank you for letting me into your hearts so many
years ago, and thank you for letting me share our story.

To the Littles:
You were the missing puzzle pieces to our family
that connect us all. You've transformed me in ways I'll never
be able to put into words. This is for you.

CONTENTS

LICENSE TO PARENT

PART ONE

WHERE IT ALL BEGAN

CHAPTER ONE

FINDING MYSELF AT THE CIA

My Unusual Path to the World of International Espionage

Contrary to popular belief, James Bond is an absolutely terrible spy. The primary goal of espionage is to gather intelligence clandestinely so that no one knows it's being done. Rather than shooting up a city or leading an elaborate car chase, the best spies in the world operate in the shadows, quietly stealing state secrets from around the world right under the noses of foreign governments. Quite frankly, if a spy has to pull out his gun or someone is chasing him, he's done something very wrong!

And don't even get me started on the "Bond girls." In real espionage, some of the best spies are not mere busty, lusty man-eaters. They're highly trained professional women who hold clandestine meetings with foreign assets all over the world, track terrorists, and write and brief the president of the United States. I should know. I was one of them.

Of course, I came into contact with many James Bond wannabes during my time at the CIA. They were certainly smooth operators, but truth be told, after several years there, I was done dating spies. The Agency attracted some of the most interesting individuals, and I was convinced I had dated them all—there was the spy who cooked me crepes in the nude, the spy who rifled through my panty drawer, and, of course, the married spy who broke my heart. I promised myself never again. And absolutely under no circumstances would I marry one.

Then I met Ryan, and I didn't stand a chance.

I didn't start off dreaming of joining the CIA. Prior to college, I didn't have much exposure to the wider world at all, let alone the world of international espionage. I grew up primarily in the Midwest in a Catholic family that alternated between being Christmas-and-Easter Catholics and regular mass attendees. I was the youngest of three kids, and my mom stayed home with my siblings and me until returning to nursing part-time when I started high school. She was born in a small town in West Virginia, and at ten years old, she moved with her parents and siblings to a farm that had been in her family for generations. That farm, and its rolling hills and roaming cattle, became a permanent fixture of my childhood and the place where I spent the majority of my holidays until I became an adult. My dad, also from West Virginia, grew up in a nearby town, and throughout my childhood he traveled domestically and internationally for his work as a safety and environmental manager at an aluminum plant.

When I was in elementary school, we moved to a suburb of Chicago, where my traditional meat-and-potatoes family values continued to take root. Each day, I traveled by bus through cornfields to school and came home to my cookie-cutter house on a cul-de-sac. I lived a largely normal Midwestern childhood, participating in extra-curricular activities like basketball and marching band. My mother played the traditional role of stay-at-home mom who volunteered as "Room Mom," sewed matching outfits for my siblings and me each holiday, and had dinner on the table by five o'clock every night. My dad carried his weight by doing the stereotypically "male" chores like mowing the lawn and taking out the trash, and he was always good for a game of PIG or HORSE in our driveway.

While I had never thought of my parents as having the most agreeable or even the happiest of marriages, divorce wasn't in my frame of reference. You can imagine my complete and utter shock when they divorced my senior year of high school, after twenty-five years of marriage. My dad and I had been touring a college a few hours away when my mom filled her car with a few essentials and left. She had rented an apartment across town and invited me to stay with her—I was the only child still living at home at the time. Even though I missed her, I chose to finish out my senior year with my dad. When the summer began, I joined my mom in her tiny apartment and began to come to grips with the fact that everything I thought I knew about marriage and family had been turned upside down.

To be clear, I knew then, like I know now, that marriage is a two-way street, and although my mom was the one who left, there was hurt and pain caused on both sides. Regardless of what happened, the desire for a traditional family ran deep for me, but as I witnessed my mom start over professionally and find her identity independent from my dad at nearly fifty years old, I began to sense the seeds of a *new* desire being sown in me to have a career and stability in my own right.

Even so, I entered Indiana University (IU) never having traveled outside the United States and with one main career ambition: to marry and have children soon after graduation. Those seeds for a professional career that were planted after my parents' divorce, however, began to grow when I started studying Swahili.

I originally applied to IU as my safety-net school. You know, the school you pick near home, in case you don't get into any of your preferred choices. I envisioned myself going out of state and had applied to several other universities, thinking I'd study journalism. However, that plan changed during my senior year of high school, when I discovered I had a talent for foreign languages. (I got perfect grades in Spanish and Latin, despite dozing off in many of my classes.) With my older brother's encouragement and guidance, I chose linguistics as my college major. Couple that with my growing interest in Africa (sparked by a high school research project and cultivated by an unhealthy obsession with *The Lion King*) and my decision to study Swahili was born. Turns out IU had one of the best African-language programs in the country. Instead of a safety net, it became my target and first choice.

Learning Swahili and taking other courses on topics like African politics and literature sparked a desire in me to truly learn—not to simply study material for straight As like I had done up to that point. I couldn't get enough of my Swahili class—so much so that I took a separate independent-study course, which consisted of reading Swahili novels with my professor. This experience gave me a deeper appreciation for the culture in addition to the language itself. I was also a volunteer language tutor on campus, where I reveled in opportunities to deconstruct the grammar of the Swahili language and help other students understand how it worked. After two years of studying Swahili, I was granted a scholarship to study in Tanzania, which only furthered my interest in Africa, as I fell in love with the people and culture. Time went on, and I enjoyed the language more and more. Soon, I started to picture myself joining the Peace Corps, perhaps as the start of a career in the humanitarian aid world. And what better way to reach people and make a difference than communicating with them in their native language?

But life had a different plan for me.

My interview with the CIA was more of a happy accident than the result of any sort of careful planning or long-held aspirations. One of my professors mentioned that a government recruiter interested in applicants with foreign language capabilities would be on campus, and I sent my résumé forward just to see if I'd hear back. I wasn't even sure that I was interested, but I figured it couldn't hurt to learn more.

My mother and new stepfather often told me that they wanted me to consider a future with the federal government, if only for the stability it would provide. As with any independent-minded twenty-one-year-old, that was enough to make me *not* want to do it. My stepfather was a senior special agent for the Department of Homeland Security and the antithesis of my father. My dad was a sociable, life-of-the-party man who enjoyed his beer, whereas my stepdad was a buttoned-up, rule-following former police officer who didn't drink alcohol or even caffeine. A lot about him screamed safety, and I suppose it made sense why my mom fell for him. Who wouldn't want a safe place to land when you're rebuilding your professional life after twenty-five years of focusing primarily on your kids?

But safety wasn't necessarily what I was looking for. Nonetheless, when I landed a generic "government interview" the same week as my Peace Corps interview, I reluctantly took their advice and showed up to the interview in my Merona suit from Target and a poorly ironed white button-down shirt.

"Hi, Christina. I'm Frank. We spoke on the phone. I'm from the Central Intelligence Agency."

WTAF.

Did I hear him right? I had mistakenly assumed this was some low-level, unimportant government entity, since the flyer didn't specify which agency the recruiter represented.

"Your foreign language skills are very impressive," Frank said.

"And I see you were a Fulbright scholar in Tanzania," he continued as he looked over my résumé and back up at me.

It turned out that my unique language capabilities were also needed by the CIA. There weren't many applicants who knew Swahili and Zulu (I studied the latter during my final year of college). They were impressed.

This was a stark contrast from my Peace Corps interview experience earlier in the week, where I was told that I didn't have any skills. This was about the time it was starting to become trendy to travel to Africa to "help people," so the Peace Corps was becoming pickier about who they chose. The CIA recruiter, on the other hand, was impressed with me, and there's no doubt the CIA has always been and continues to be very picky about who it chooses.

Frank went on to tell me about the position. He said I'd have the opportunity to use my Africa expertise and foreign language skills to influence US policy, and I'd even travel to Africa on a regular basis. I could barely contain my excitement. I couldn't believe I almost skipped out on this opportunity entirely.

A few weeks later, I received a job offer from the CIA, contingent on a background investigation and security clearance. I filled out pages and pages of biographical information, and security investigators began interviewing my family members, friends, friends of friends, and neighbors. Was I a patriot? Did I use drugs? Had I ever hacked into any computer systems? Did I pirate music? Was I a trustworthy person? Thankfully, as a fresh-out-of-college twenty-one-year-old who had traveled to only one foreign country and had very little life experience, I breezed through the process, with the exception of the polygraph examination.

I underwent extensive medical and psychological testing and not one, but two polygraph examinations. I failed my first four-hour polygraph on account of suspicions that I was a drug smuggler, all because of a pot muffin I consumed during a layover in Amsterdam and failed to tell them about. (I blame it on the Catholic guilt. That shit runs deep.) Luckily, I had another opportunity the following day. (I later learned that the polygraph is useful only as an interrogation tool, and it's only as reliable as the polygrapher who is conducting it.)

I passed the second attempt with flying colors, and four months later, I found myself sitting in a room with about fifty others taking an oath to spy for our country. Some of my fellow recruits were motivated to join out of a fiercely patriotic desire to serve their country. Others were thrill seekers looking for adventure. Many were fulfilling a lifelong dream to be like James Bond. Strangely, I was there because of my love of a foreign land.

I was excited, but not for the first time I found myself wondering: *What am I doing here?*

Fast-forward several years: I was working at the CIA as one of the most senior analysts on the East Africa account, which aligned perfectly with the language and subject matter expertise I'd brought with me from my university studies. Despite my initial fish-out-of-water unease, I discovered that once I was in a professional environment where I excelled at something I loved, I had more career ambitions than I'd previously thought.

I lived and breathed my job—and I was good at it. It turns out that most of the work at the CIA wasn't in-the-field spy tradecraft, at least not in my directorate, the Directorate of Intelligence, or DI, which is now called the Directorate of Analysis. It was about writing, briefing, and critical thinking. I spent my days analyzing swaths of intelligence reports that had been collected by operations officers in the field, writing intelligence assessments for the US president and other US policymakers, and briefing those assessments to US leaders. The very cautious, careful, detail-oriented qualities that had made me good at school made me shine at the Agency. As my career thrived, I didn't really have time for serious romance, although it hadn't always been like that.

Paul and I met on our first day of orientation at the CIA. He was tall, clean-cut, and attractive. We both brought packed lunches and agreed to find a table to sit together. I learned over ham-and-cheese sandwiches that he'd grown up in a small farm town in Iowa. He was stoic and calm—robotic, even—and I wasn't surprised when he told me he was an engineer and had been hired into the Agency's Directorate of Science and Technology (DS&T). Learning he was an engineer fascinated me, probably because it was something I felt I could never do. Paul told me he had always wanted to be an astronaut but due to a heart condition he'd had as an infant, he wouldn't pass the physical requirements to travel in space. He decided to do the next best thing—become a rocket scientist.

As I sat across from Paul and listened to him speak, I mentally checked off boxes in my head: Successful career? Check. Attractive?

Check. Intelligent? Check. Ambitious? Check. It was only day one and I had found myself the perfect boyfriend, and dare I say, the perfect *husband*.

After only three months, Paul and I moved in together. I felt like I had all my ducks in a row—the successful career and now the right man. And what's more? Even my mom loved Paul. He was a smart, stable man with an ability to support me—qualities she emphasized were important in a partner. She also continued to stress the importance of having my own career, just in case. I trusted my mom's advice, and with her approval, I was even more enamored of Paul.

I stayed that way for nearly two years, until I reached a point when I realized it wasn't working. Something was missing. With Paul, I was just . . . existing. The passionate, driven woman I knew was disappearing. I couldn't put my finger on it—and he had yet to put a ring on it—but something told me he wasn't the One. I ended things abruptly in a phone call from an undisclosed location, where I was on a temporary-duty assignment for work.

"I just don't think we should be together anymore," I said into the phone on the floor of my hotel room. On my finger, I twirled the ring he had bought me before I left town nearly four weeks earlier. It wasn't an engagement ring, but it felt like it was a precursor to one that would be coming fairly soon.

"Are you okay? What's going on?" he asked.

"Yes, I'm fine," I said, part of me wanting to take back everything I had just said. But as I looked over at my hotel bed, I had flashbacks from the night before. Clothes strewn across the floor, laughter, touching . . . There were some gaps, but what I knew for sure was that I'd brought my colleague back to my hotel room after a work happy hour. He and I had been flirting for weeks, and I was drawn to his passion for Africa, one that I, of course, shared. Perhaps it was inevitable that we'd find ourselves in bed together.

"It's just that the time away has given me some perspective," I said coolly into the phone as I took off the ring and set it on the nightstand. There was no going back at this point. I couldn't tell Paul what I had done—it would hurt him too much. And how could I really love him if I was willing to do what I'd done?

Two weeks later, I flew home to Northern Virginia, where I had to face the reality of my rash decision. The fact that I felt it was the right thing to do didn't make it any easier when it came time to do the dreaded "that's mine, this is yours" at our shared apartment in Fairfax. Like any good friend, Marissa, my oldest and best friend, was on the first flight to help me with the logistics of moving and, more than anything, for moral support.

"What did I do wrong?" Paul asked as we went through kitchen drawers.

"Nothing," I told him.

That was the hardest part. Paul *hadn't* done anything wrong. He had checked all the boxes; he had everything I thought I wanted in a husband—on paper. The problem was that I realized I didn't want a paper husband. I wanted a real one.

But not quite yet.

From then on, I dated some (including those aforementioned colleagues at the CIA), but it had never turned into anything serious or worthwhile. Mostly, I lived the life of a carefree single woman. Every few months, my just-as-ambitious teammate and close friend, Jen, and I treated ourselves to a long weekend in Las Vegas, where we spent ample time lying by the pool, going to clubs, and recharging at the spa. But even then, work always came first: My best paper was one she and I outlined over drinks on one such weekend. (Those cryptic notes on my cocktail napkin became a baseline assessment for my team on a political kingmaker in Kenya and his rise to power.)

It felt *good* to be good at this. It felt great to succeed. In our tipsier moments, Jen and I cheekily wondered what it might be like to not be so driven.

"What if we didn't care so much? Like, what if we just did the bare minimum we needed to do to get our paychecks?" I asked Jen.

"You mean, what if we were mediocre?" she asked.

"Exactly."

We laughed. Not a chance.

We "clinked" our plastic poolside cocktail cups, vowing to each other that we'd never stop climbing the ladder at the Agency. Our goal was to be the youngest women to reach the Senior Analytic Service, an esteemed position for only the most experienced and exceptional of analysts. It wasn't simply a promotion—although that did come along with the title—entrance was permitted only after an extensive application and interview process. We knew that with careful planning, strict discipline, and hard work, we could do it.

We were aware that meant there were parts of our lives that might suffer, which sometimes meant our love lives. And for the most part, we were okay with that. What we weren't okay with were our married colleagues who acted like they had it all figured out. You know the type—the ones who look at you and say, "Oh don't worry, Christina, you'll find someone." Jen and I liked to call these people the Smug Marrieds. Oh, and the ones with kids were even worse. Not only did they have it all figured out, but they expected us, as young singles, to stay late to sign off on papers they wrote because *we* didn't have families at home, so whatever *we* were going home to was less important. (I'd later come to regret this attitude and even apologize to a colleague who was juggling her career and a new baby at the time.) But the truth was, work really *was* the most important thing in our lives, and we were okay with that. What we didn't understand was why it wasn't number one in everyone else's lives too.

Spending most of our waking hours at work meant meeting someone outside the CIA bubble was highly unlikely for us, and for this reason and others, it was common for many CIA officers to date from within. After all, it was easier to date someone who understood the secretive lifestyle. Dating another CIA officer meant they understood when you couldn't give more details about the paper you were working on or your last-minute trip to a covert location. More than that, they had already been through the same extensive security and psychological checks that you had. Free vetting, so to speak. In some ways, this made dating simpler, but in other ways, it made CIA Headquarters an incestuous pool, filled with operations officers practicing their, at times, *manipulative* tradecraft . . . with you as the target.

To be completely honest, my personal life was often at odds with my professional life. At work, I was a buttoned-up analyst, relying on research to make very careful analytic judgments, whereas off the clock, I had a passionate, shoot-first-ask-questions-later, work-hard-play-hard mentality (Vegas, baby!). Work was an area of my life that I could control. My personal life was where I let loose.

My deeply ingrained desire to find the One underpinned a lot of the admittedly poor choices I made with regard to romance. Instead of the data-driven approach to decision-making I took at work, my choices regarding affairs of the heart were often fueled by my good friends chardonnay and tequila. You could say I was a little bit of a wreck at times. Think Fleabag meets Carrie Mathison . . . but more stable. Or so I'd like to think. After years of this pattern, I decided it was time for a change. I had been burned by men at the CIA too many times, and enough was enough. I was nearing thirty, and I had finally begun to settle in as the confident, successful single career woman I was, and that inner monologue telling me to find a husband finally began to quiet down.

Enter Ryan.

CHAPTER TWO

FALLING FOR MR. BOND

And Becoming a Stepmom in the Process

We had only a few minutes before our break ended and class would start up again, and I wanted to be sure to meet those two operations officers sitting across the room. I was preparing for a new rotational assignment in the coming months, and I knew these two would be posted at my same CIA field Station. Nervous about entering a new division of the CIA, I knew I would need as many friends on this new team as I could get.

I introduced myself to the first officer and kept it short and sweet. He was friendly enough, and any other time, I may have spent more time talking with him to build team rapport. But I wanted to make my way to the other operations officer. He was the one who'd caught my eye.

He was tall with a tan complexion, a scruffy beard, and a shaved head. He had big brown almond-shaped eyes—the kind you could get lost in. He was dressed in a plaid button-down shirt and a khaki-colored Filson blazer. Everything about him screamed masculinity. Adventure.

Our introduction was brief—we couldn't have shared more than a few words before the instructor called us back to our seats. We were in an Agency-required training course, specifically for officers departing for a Permanent Change of Station (PCS). This would be my first tour away from Headquarters, in which I would spend the majority of the next three years away from my desk, conducting my own operational meetings, a stark contrast from the analytic world I had grown used to over the years.

For the rest of the day, I stole glances at Ryan from across the room whenever I could. I found myself daydreaming about what a life with him would be like. It was full of exploration, and for a second, I felt like I had gotten a glimpse into my future. I brushed those thoughts aside and told myself to stay focused. I had a tendency to get carried away with romantic fantasies, and the last thing I needed when I arrived at my new post was to jump into a relationship right away. And with an operations officer, no less!

When I arrived at the CIA Station two months later, Ryan wasted no time in pursuing me. We met briefly in person again at the office, and it wasn't long before he was pinging me on the CIA's internal instant messenger. He talked about archery and skiing, and he promised to teach me both sometime soon, if I was interested.

I was about the least adventurous person I knew, and the thought of skiing genuinely frightened me. I may have made impulsive choices in my love life, but when it came to general safety, I was about as rule-following and risk-averse as a person could be. But with Ryan as my teacher, I felt willing to try just about anything. You could say it was his up-for-anything demeanor that put me at ease, but perhaps I was just so attracted to him that I didn't want him to know how boring I could be. As someone who had poured her heart and soul into her career for years at this point, I hadn't made all that much time—okay, any at all—for hobbies. It was time to change that, and he seemed like just the right person with whom I could start to develop some interests outside the Agency.

The catch? He was divorced with three children.

For whatever reason, this didn't send me running for the hills. Maybe it was the cute, hand-drawn pictures from his kids that adorned his cubicle that softened my heart. Or maybe it was his rugged sex appeal. Whatever the case, I happily accepted his invitation to go on a date.

That Saturday, we met for lunch at a local Italian restaurant called Angelo's. We laughed for hours; it was as if I was talking to someone I had known my whole life. After a few hours of Italian food, we moved across the street for dessert. Like any good operations officer, Ryan was a smooth talker and had a variety of interests. He wowed me with his tales of baking artisan bread from scratch, speaking four different languages, playing the Irish pennywhistle, and leather making. It was the first time I had encountered a man who could easily shift from discussing medieval knives to his favorite dish to cook from Julia Child's *Mastering the Art of French Cooking*.

Sure, most operations officers had a variety of interests and were quite suave, but there was something different about Ryan. I got the sense that his interests were genuine and not created solely in an effort to assist his espionage efforts. He was truly multifaceted, which no doubt made him incredibly successful at his job.

While we both worked in the CIA, our work experience there couldn't have been more different. Ryan was an operations officer in the Directorate of Operations (DO), which meant he recruited foreign targets who had access to information of interest and devised other spooky operations to collect intelligence. For example, he once took up scuba diving as a hobby just to get close to a target with vital information to US national security. He was one of the very few CIA officers who actually had gone to the Farm, the CIA's covert training facility, and successfully completed formal training to be a spy. He'd spent time abroad, working in countries in Europe, Asia, and the Middle East, and he had training in human intelligence and things like weapons, escape and evasion techniques, and covert communications.

In other words, the guy really was James Bond. But not in the unrealistic Hollywood or chauvinistic ways. Ryan was the real deal.

He was also operating from a totally different playbook than I was. We both worked for the CIA, but my career to that point had largely been spent analyzing intelligence reports at a desk with occasional trips to Africa. Both of us were highly trained in our respective areas of intelligence expertise, of course. But Ryan's type of fieldwork placed a high priority on being nimble and agile and at times taking calculated risks.

While my directorate, the DI, was full of experts who were laser-focused on a single subject matter—knowing everything there was to know about a specific region, like the Horn of Africa, for example—the DO comprised individuals who met the description "a mile wide and an inch deep." I was a specialist, but the DO was full of generalists who had to be good at a lot of different, disparate tasks: they might meet with an asset with expertise on nuclear issues one day and an asset with access to a terrorist network in a different part of the world the next. They needed to be able to speak to and understand an array of topics to successfully collect impactful intelligence. While we in the DI liked to turn our noses up at their lack of deep expertise, I quickly learned while working alongside them that they were just as intelligent. More than that, there was something impressive about their ability to shift naturally from topic to topic and, for example, memorize an hours-long dinner conversation in enough detail to write up once they returned to the office (which I saw my DO colleagues do on more than one occasion).

It was true Ryan had impressed me in all these ways at work, but I was even more impressed when I met his three children and saw the way he parented. It was about three months into our dating relationship when he told me he was ready to introduce me to Hannah, Hunter, and Lena. I knew it was a big step for him. It was for me too.

Thoughts raced through my mind as I drove to meet them for the first time. *Will the kids like me? I'm not good with kids—that's my sister's thing. She's the first-grade teacher; I'm the power-suit-wearing workaholic.*

I kept repeating my friend Marissa's advice in my head when I'd told her my concerns.

"It's okay if it's too much for you," she said. "No harm, no foul. You will have given it a shot. If you decide to walk away, that's just fine."

After I arrived at Ryan's home, we all drove to a pumpkin patch together. It was almost Halloween, and I'd brought the kids treat bags, complete with candy corn, fun-size candy bars, and edible mustaches. (When in doubt, bring sweets.) Much to my surprise, the day went smoothly—with the exception being my decision to wear brand-new Tory Burch flats in a corn maze.

Not only did everything at the pumpkin patch go well, it also felt *natural*, oddly enough. Just in case I wasn't already falling in love with Ryan, I had the chance to see him be the most incredible father to three little ones who were tiny mirror images of him. Hannah, the oldest of the kids at nine years old, was quiet, yet curious. Hunter had just turned eight, and it was clear he had Ryan's adventurous spirit and interest in the outdoors. Lena was only six, and when I looked at her sweet face, somehow I knew she'd be the first one I'd win over. The whole experience was like looking into a crystal ball and knowing the kind of father your boyfriend would be to your kids someday— a benefit most women don't get before marrying someone.

While I could tell right off the bat that Ryan was an amazing dad, there were a few things he did that caught my attention and felt different to me. For instance, I noticed that he didn't always have eyes on the kids when we were walking through the elaborate corn maze. He gave them a fairly long leash as we navigated our way through, and as if he were the head of the von Trapp family in *The Sound of Music*, he'd whistle like a bird or a cricket almost, and they would promptly return. It was a similar dynamic when we entered the gift shop; they wandered about and even made their own purchases. And I didn't sense any sort of worry in Ryan's face when he couldn't see the kids. In fact, he was at ease and appeared in control at all times, albeit sometimes from afar. Even so, I wasn't sure that's how *I* would parent. The idea of not seeing my kids in a store seemed scary enough, but in an actual *maze* that is meant to make people get lost? Well, that seemed like a little *too* much autonomy to me.

Over the next year, Ryan and I spent every weekend together, and most of those weekends we had the kids. I noticed early on that they were more adventurous and well-rounded than I was at their age, and frankly, any other children I knew. They were active, doing everything from riding motorcycles to hiking mountains to playing tag at the park. I didn't know any other kids who rode motorcycles at their ages; just the thought of putting kids on them made me break out in a nervous sweat. Now at six, eight, and ten years old, they exercised independence beyond their years when they pulled out their leather money pouches to make purchases themselves. Sometimes those purchases were under Ryan's watchful eye, like at the pumpkin patch. But other times, shockingly to me, they would go shopping alone—like when Ryan dropped them off curbside at the grocery store to run in and pick up a few items. They talked about what they would take with them to a desert island or what they'd need for the zombie apocalypse, and I was always surprised at how much knowledge they had about tools and survival in general.

"Pretend there's a zombie apocalypse, and we're the only people left in the whole world. Let's make a list of the things we'd need to survive," Hannah said to her younger brother and sister as she pulled out her notepad.

"Flashlight . . . rope . . . machete . . ." Hunter began to list off items.

"Water . . . Sour Patch Kids . . ." Lena, the youngest, playfully added.

"Oh man, this would be so cool if it happened," said Hunter.

At first, it seemed odd to me that their favorite conversation topics revolved around end-of-the-world scenarios and compiling lists of the necessary survival tools, especially when most kids their age were playing video games or talking about their middle school crush. But I quickly realized when your dad was a CIA spy—or, more accurately, when your dad was Ryan—this wasn't odd at all. It was the norm.

I had no doubt that Ryan's parenting techniques were unique and at least partly responsible for how exceptional his kids were.

Their time living abroad for Ryan's CIA tours also gave them early exposure to many different cultures, which certainly gave them a leg up on your typical American kid. At the same time, I found myself grappling with the amount of autonomy he gave them and the exposure to what I felt were mature topics at very young ages. Why should kids be worrying about an apocalypse and what they'd need to survive before they were even ten years old? I considered attributing some of my concerns to lapses in his judgment or his being a single dad, but the more time we spent together, the more I began to realize that these were carefully thought-out parenting techniques.

The months went on, and just before our second Christmas together, Ryan proposed. We had a short engagement—only three months long. I'm pretty sure everyone thought I was knocked up, but when nine months passed and there still wasn't a baby, I guess they realized we were just two people who knew what we wanted and didn't see the point in spending a year or longer planning a wedding. Prior to meeting Ryan, I had always planned on having a year-long engagement, at a minimum. What can I say? I suppose his spontaneity was already rubbing off on me.

Once we married, I was thrust into the world of parenting. There's nothing like jumping right into parenting tweens. It doesn't leave much room for error since they are old enough to notice—and remember—all of your mistakes. I followed Ryan's lead and slowly came into my own as a stepmother. Over time, I began learning what made his kids so unique: since they were young, he had been teaching them certain CIA techniques that he believed would keep them safe and set them apart from their peers. More than anything, Ryan sought to instill in his kids a spirit of adventure and knowledge of the world that he hoped would help shape them into versatile, successful adults. This fascinated me.

But in some ways, it also scared me.

I knew in theory that the training both of us had undergone to prepare for our intelligence work was good training for life too. Independence, anticipating danger, having a flexible mind-set—these are all vital life skills for kids as well as adults. Ryan's somewhat unconventional parenting strategies were proving successful in teaching the kids these abilities.

But in practice, I was concerned about giving young people that much autonomy and responsibility, especially these three children who I had grown to love. What if something happened to them? What if they couldn't handle the long leash that Ryan was offering them at what seemed to me a very young age? When I imagined the type of parent I'd be someday, I had always anticipated I'd subscribe to more of the unapologetically helicopter variety.

Then we had a baby, and that changed everything.

CHAPTER THREE

ADOPTING A CIA-BASED PARENTING STYLE

How Birthing a Child Prompted Me to Get On Board

Up until our son Ari's birth, I had very much parented from the sidelines. Being a stepmom can be tricky; I was constantly aware of the fact that my connections with Ryan's children, who we began calling the Bigs, weren't underpinned with blood or even a bond from birth. I worried that any misstep could jeopardize the carefully built relationships I had worked so hard to form with each one of them. Moreover, I wanted to respect the norms Ryan had already established with the Bigs, so sometimes if I was skeptical of something he did or didn't do, it was easier for me not to question it, particularly in front of the kids.

Ryan and I had also agreed that it was important for us to have a united front when it came to parenting, or at least appear that way in front of the kids. We agreed that we'd always have each other's back, and any disagreements would be handled privately. (Of course, it doesn't always happen that way because life isn't perfect. And neither are we!) But when it came to some things, like how the Bigs had been raised up until I came into the picture, I often subscribed to the mind-set of "That train has already left the station." I filed things away that I planned to address with Ryan later when we had a baby—namely motorcycles, knives, and movies. My concerns were surrounding activities that didn't seem safe or appropriate for children, primarily because I hadn't been exposed to them in my childhood. I had also been a worrier for as long as I could remember—no doubt stemming from my father's career in safety management and my mother's constant worrying—so when I pictured myself as a parent, I assumed my style would lean heavily toward a risk-averse approach. I had never considered what it might look like to introduce these topics to children in a safe way that set them up to be more security-conscious and ultimately safer.

After Ari's birth, what I used to consider a slightly above-average amount of worrying turned into full-on postpartum anxiety. During his newborn days, I lay awake even on nights when he slept, as rare as those were at the time, constantly checking his breathing and heart rate stats on an app on my phone that was connected via Bluetooth to a special sock on his foot. The Bigs were anxious to hold him any chance they got, but every fiber of my being screamed out when he wasn't in my arms. I loved the Bigs so much, but at Ari's birth some sort of primal biology had taken over, and I was in straight-up Mama Bear mode. Ryan tried to assure me that they just wanted to help—they were so excited about their baby brother, he'd tell me. But I didn't see it that way. And the fact that I often nursed him in private upstairs (who wants to learn to nurse in front of their middle-school-aged stepson?) only strengthened the bubble I had put myself in with Ari.

When I returned to work following four months of maternity leave, I struggled being away from him all day long. In addition to the juggling act of scheduling time to pump between meetings multiple times throughout the day, I worried about Ari's safety and constantly checked my phone for any sort of picture updates on the day-care's app. I fully intended to become a working mother—my old Midwest dreams of being a stay-at-home mom had all but disappeared by this point because I genuinely loved having a career and couldn't imagine who I'd be without one. But I surprised myself when after only two months back in the office, I decided to stay home full-time after all. No matter how much I tried, I couldn't shake the feeling that I was missing out on milestones with Ari, and I accepted the fact that for the first time in my life, something—or *someone*, rather—had bumped my career out of its number one spot.

I took on my new role as stay-at-home mom and stepmom with gusto. I began to find satisfaction in things like preparing dinner in the slow cooker before heading out the door for an early-morning exercise class with Ari in tow . . . or when I finally mastered nursing him while wearing him in the baby carrier around the house . . . or on the days when I timed Ari's nap just right so that I could pick up Hunter from basketball practice. These may sound like seemingly small accomplishments, but to me, a sleep-deprived new mother trying to balance a newborn and preteens, they felt enormous. And just as I was beginning to feel like I was finally getting the hang of things, they changed. With only a few days' notice, we learned that Hannah and Lena would be moving in with us full-time (Hunter had already been living with us for two years, and we had been trying to move the girls into our house ever since), meaning I had more mouths to feed and more schedules to juggle. And in 2018, our family grew even more when we added our daughter Gigi into the mix. Together with Ari, the two of them make up what we call the Littles. With five children at home in very different life stages, I found that remaining on the parenting sidelines was no longer an option for me. Instead of merely observing Ryan's parenting style, I knew it was time to become an active participant and implementer. And to be honest, I knew I needed help with my anxiety. I didn't want to parent from a place of fear, and I knew that adopting Ryan's mind-set, to an extent that felt natural to me, would help me to instead parent from a place of knowledge and strength.

"I feel like I need to take a more active role when it comes to parenting," I said one night as Ryan and I were getting into bed.

"What do you mean? You're already very involved," he said.

"Well, yeah, but I just kind of follow your lead with the Bigs. Now that all three of them live with us full-time, and we have Ari and Gigi, I want to make sure we're on the same page with everything," I said.

"Of course."

"What I mean is, I like a lot of the things you've done with the Bigs, but I'm also not entirely on board with some of them . . . and we may want to do some things differently with the Littles." It wasn't the first time I had mentioned this to Ryan, but previously it was more in passing or even in a joking sort of way.

"I know, I know. You don't like knives and motorcycles," he said as though it wasn't anything new to him.

"Listen, I need to understand why you do things the way you do, and maybe I'll come around on those. But I want to have a say in how we parent too. It's not just you anymore—now the kids have *two* parents who worked at the CIA, and we have much different perspectives."

This prompted Ryan and me to agree on a parenting style together that drew heavily on *both* of our experiences at the CIA—his clandestine operational side and my analytic side. I had already brought a sense of fashion for his girls, who were being dressed by a single dad who (admittedly) had no idea what he was doing, and now I was ready to bring more of my measured, analytic approach to our family. It wasn't long before the Bigs started bypassing Ryan and coming straight to me for help with their homework (and that was just fine with him!). I also quickly became Hannah's go-to when she thought Ryan was living too much in the gray, because she knows I am naturally a very structured rule follower, much like she is, and that I'll give her sound advice.

Sometimes our approach goes smoothly. Once in a while, it doesn't (and I'll tell you about that too!). While some things initially gave me pause, like motorcycle riding or whittling sticks, by and large the other concepts he taught the kids—like security aware-ness, communication strategies, and financial responsibility—resonated with me from the get-go. He's helped me transfer my CIA skills and knowledge to commonsense parenting, finding an overlap between two periods of my life that once felt so very different to me. We like to call it "the CIA way of parenting."

Together with Ryan, I've broken down our respective CIA train-ing into rudimentary concepts that our children can understand and build upon as they grow up, with the primary focus on raising strong, security-conscious, independent kids. We want them to be able to make quick, proactive, and commonsense decisions, whether they are in the classroom or out with friends to see a movie. Above all else, we want them to have a prepared mind-set, an ability to think critically, and the power to remain calm in an anxious situation.

We're currently experiencing an epidemic of helicopter parents like we've never seen, with kids who have "failed to launch." We'd argue that this has been caused in part by kids who haven't been given the tools to succeed on their own. I want to help you learn these tools so your kids can become independent and self-reliant, all while staying safe.

It's a journey. And it's one we're still on, every day. But my hope is that by sharing our story of how we've incorporated these espionage techniques into our parenting style, you too can learn how to apply these skills to set your kids up to be strong, safe, and independent. We all want our kids to develop the tools to survive—and hopefully thrive—in this fast-changing world. After all, the CIA trains its employees to be equipped to deal with just about anything. Why shouldn't parents strive to do the same for their kids?

PART TWO

PUTTING IT INTO PRACTICE

CHAPTER FOUR

BE PREPARED

How to Survive the Everyday
to the Most Extreme Circumstances

"Oh, this definitely goes into the 'keep' pile," Ryan said as he held up a small green satchel in the air. It was a few years before Ari's arrival, and we were unpacking our belongings in our first shared home, which we had just bought together. The house was built in 1949, and while it was definitely what I'd call a fixer-upper, we fell in love with the character it had and pictured creating memories with our growing family for years to come.

"Why do we need that tiny bag?" I asked.

"It was one of the kids' adventure bags . . . we can use it again for our baby," Ryan told me. At the time, I had no idea what "adventure bag" meant, but it sounded relatively harmless to me, so I said okay, sure, and we packed it away until we needed it. Frankly, I would have said yes to saving just about anything for the future baby Ryan spoke of. Just hearing him say the words *our* and *baby* together in the same sentence made it feel real to me—like he was speaking it into existence. A tiny wooden desk that this imaginary child may or may not write at someday? Of course! A little red antique chair to pair with the desk? Let's keep it. The truth was, I often struggled to find my place as a new stepmom, especially on holidays like Mother's Day, and I yearned for the day that I'd birth a child. In fact, there was a time early in our dating relationship when I didn't know if it would even be possible.

"Oh shoot, I better take my birth control pill," I said to Ryan one evening as we were brushing our teeth before bed.

"Oh, you don't need to worry about that," he said.

Ryan then told me that the reason I didn't need to worry was because he had gotten a vasectomy after the birth of his third child. I can still remember the shock and utter devastation I felt after the words came out of his mouth. And the way he said it so casually infuriated me.

"You didn't think this was something you should have mentioned months ago?" I asked, trying to keep my cool.

"It's reversible," he said with equal parts nonchalance and optimism.

I clung to those two words over the next two and a half years as we went through doctor's appointments where we were called a sterile couple, a surgery that reversed the decision he'd made long ago, and ultimately the joyous, although incredibly painful and torturous, birth of our son.

Fast-forward another two years and there Ryan sat at our kitchen table next to two-year-old Ari.

"Ooh, what else do you have in your adventure bag?" Ryan asked Ari. "Let's look in it and see."

"Let's see!" Ari agreed excitedly.

"Your very own flashlight!" Ryan exclaimed.

"No way!" Ari said as he reached for it.

This continued as Ryan introduced each item to Ari, one by one, that he had carefully chosen for Ari's very first adventure bag: a whistle, an emergency blanket, a glow stick, a compass, flint and steel, and Band-Aids. Next, he allowed Ari to pick out some of his favorite snacks to include for the hike we planned for later that afternoon. While our toddler viewed this as a fun exercise in preparing for the day's hike, what he didn't know was that Ryan was already taking another page from his CIA training in beginning to teach Ari the importance of being prepared.

Indeed, woven throughout all the training at the CIA is this idea of being prepared. In the event that CIA officers can't get away from danger (more on that later), they need to be ready to survive just about anything—from terrorist attacks on the US embassy to local uprisings to natural disasters, to name a few possibilities. And these *are* real possibilities. As an Africa analyst, it wasn't uncommon for me to hear firsthand about dangerous situations my colleagues had experienced in countries across the continent—from the 1998 US embassy bombings in Kenya and Tanzania to coups d'état in West Africa, and everything in between.

In order to survive scenarios like bombings and natural disasters, CIA officers need to have the skills and supplies to survive if the ship goes down. Operations officers at the CIA are taught survival skills early in their training, which includes everything from land navigation to first aid. They're put through the toughest and most strenuous training scenarios in hopes that what they encounter in real life will never be as difficult. While most of my specialized training at the CIA focused on analytic skills like writing, briefing, and critical thinking, as you may have gleaned by now, Ryan's training was very different.

-RYAN-

LAND NAVIGATION AT THE FARM

I had been following my coordinates and walking for about twenty minutes in the woods by this point. I knew I was close—it should be right in front of me. But it wasn't. *Where the hell is this thing?* I thought to myself. I carefully retraced my steps and tried to find it again, but with no luck. After frantically running around for another ten minutes, I finally found the barrel—a mere twenty yards away on the other side of a tree. I hurriedly got my next coordinates and made my way to the next barrel. I continued on to the third, fourth, and then finally the fifth and last barrel. At this point, I knew I was cutting it close. I sprinted back to the barracks; I had made it just in time.

I was taking part in a complex and demanding exercise at the Farm, in which my classmates and I were each expected to find hidden fifty-gallon drums in the woods, armed only with a Suunto compass (which I have to this day), a paper map, and geo-coordinates. The Farm instructors taught us how to quickly compensate for magnetic declination (i.e., true north versus magnetic north) on our compasses depending on what area of the world we were operating in—something I had never really understood before this course.

Having earned the rank of Eagle Scout in Boy Scouts when I was seventeen, I knew how to use a compass and read a map. I had also earned my orienteering merit badge. I thought I was well versed in these techniques and understood how to find my way around. This couldn't be further from the truth. As it turned out,

I hadn't really known how to do these things until my training at the Farm. In fact, it was around this time that I came to the disappointing realization that the Boy Scouts hadn't fully prepared me like I had thought. I determined right then and there that my kids would always be prepared, no matter what life threw at them.

In addition to these land-navigation skills, which are extremely important for CIA officers serving in remote and dangerous areas like Afghanistan, Ryan's training at the Farm also included first aid and basic medical skills and emergency-response techniques. One of the key focus points the CIA emphasized repeatedly was how to properly apply a tourniquet to stop bleeding and save lives. While this may seem like a fundamental skill, the instructors stressed that its importance could not be overstated. To give you some perspective, in the 1998 embassy bombings in Kenya and Tanzania, more than two hundred were killed and approximately five thousand were wounded—any and all people who had first aid skills, including CPR, likely would have been needed. But, of course, these basic survival skills aren't just useful for CIA officers. Do your kids know how to give proper CPR to an adult? What about a baby? Do they know what a tourniquet is and where to place it?

While a terrorist attack may sound like an extreme example when it comes to what our kids might experience, preparing them ahead of time gives them the best chance to survive any scenario, even ones that may seem improbable. We do that by giving them the tools and knowledge to endure everything, from the mundane act of forgetting their house key and being stuck outside until Mom gets home to natural disasters. Similar to CIA training, the idea here is to prepare your kids for emergencies with the expectation and hope that they'll never need to utilize these skills.

There are so many ways to view survival skills, and you can choose what you want to focus on with your kids based on your personal interests. It's important that you teach your kids that if something were to happen, whether it's a natural disaster, war, pandemic, or the collapse of the economy, the flow of goods and services may stop, and when it does, chaos will ensue. In fact, goods start disappearing from the shelves sometimes at the first inkling of an imminent disaster. Take, for example, the start of the COVID-19 pandemic in early 2020. We watched as people aggressively sought items like toilet paper, paper towels, disinfectant, rice, beans, flour, yeast, and so on. For these very real reasons, we keep emergency food storage and supplies in our home. We live near a river, so we have water filtration devices on hand to ensure we'll always have access to clean water. We also keep a large supply of small items that would work well for trading purposes in the event money is no longer available—think basic necessities as well as vices such as cigarettes, small bottles of alcohol, chewing tobacco, and the like.

When it comes down to it, most humans don't know basic survival skills because we are a culture that relies heavily on modern amenities and technology. We don't know how to take care of ourselves in the same way the human race once did. By and large, people don't know how to do things like churn butter, make soap, garden, forge metal, or use herbs for healing sickness, for example.

If you're a doctor or a nurse, you might choose to focus on teaching your kids the importance of having medical supplies on hand, which would also likely be unavailable in a situation in which the flow of goods and services was interrupted or stopped. You may choose to focus on teaching them homeopathic ways to treat medical conditions. If you enjoy camping, focus on teaching your kids how to start a fire and how to survive in the wilderness. Maybe the idea of food storage resonates with you. Or perhaps you'd like to start your own garden so that if food becomes unavailable, your family could grow your own.

During the COVID-19 pandemic, we saw an uptick in gardening, including many learning to garden for the first time, drawing comparisons to the victory gardens grown during WWI and WWII.[1] If you live somewhere rural, you may also consider purchasing chickens so that you regularly have access to fresh eggs. However this ends up looking for your family, the most important thing to remember is that teaching your kids proper food-storage techniques or gardening skills is a great way to equip them with more survival skills. If and when another emergency situation comes upon us, you and your kids are that much more prepared. And if the COVID-19 pandemic has taught us anything, it's that emergency food storage and preparedness is no longer for the weird doomsday preppers. It's smart and absolutely necessary. Because as we all now know firsthand, the unlikely can become a *very real* possibility quite quickly.

Let me be clear when I say that I'm not suggesting at any point that you hoard goods. Specifically, I want to emphasize that you shouldn't run out and stockpile supplies, especially after an emergency has already begun or appears imminent. Yes, there will always be people who do this and, for example, take personal protective equipment (PPE) from the health care workers who need it most, but that doesn't need to be you. By thinking and planning ahead, you can avoid having to run out at the last minute with the masses.

Shifting gears a bit, when thinking about survival skills, you may gravitate toward weapons and the desire to defend yourself. CIA officers take part in advanced weapons training, but weapons aren't just for defending yourself. They can also be used to hunt for food, if necessary. For example, Ryan taught the Bigs archery using a long-bow when they were fairly young, knowing that it can be an excellent way to obtain food, if necessary. The Bigs were especially interested in archery when I met them because it was around the time the first Hunger Games movie came out. Hannah, in particular, loved it because she read the books and identified with Katniss—as much for her long brown hair as her desire for adventure, not to mention her penchant for protecting her younger siblings. This was another example of Ryan making survival fun and adventurous for the Bigs, all while knowing he was equipping them with a vital life skill that could one day prove useful in an emergency or self-defense scenario. Years later, Lena blew her classmates out of the water when they did a unit on archery in her seventh-grade PE class. Many of the other students—especially the girls—had never been exposed to archery, while Lena was hitting bull's-eye after bull's-eye and even putting the boys to shame. It's skills like these that can make your kids stand out while also preparing them for the unknown.

The reality is that basic survival knowledge that humans have known for thousands of years is a lost art. Find what it is that you want your kids to know. Once you choose what you want to emphasize to them, it's time to develop how you'll introduce these topics.

Start with Adventure

How do you take terrifying concepts like how to survive a major natural disaster and explain them to your kids in a way that doesn't scare them? Start by taking a step back and thinking about the skills your kids would need in order to survive those scenarios. For example, Ryan has ingrained the idea of survival in the Bigs—and now the Littles—since they were young. He began with small hiking adventure bags, filled with things like Band-Aids, a compass, a flashlight, snacks, and juice boxes. The idea of giving young kids their very own emergency bag and making it sound fun had never occurred to me, but seeing Ari get so into it confirmed for me what a great tactic this was.

As the Bigs grew older, this idea evolved into survival bags or what we call "go bags." When arriving at a CIA Station for a tour, each officer is given a go bag to keep in their car or under their desk in case of emergency. We've adapted that idea for our family, and it's a natural next step for the kids once they've moved on from their adventure bags. Each of our cars is equipped with a go bag, which includes survival gear like matches, blankets, ponchos, kindling, a tarp, flashlights, batteries, maps, a machete, a knife, pepper spray, a first aid kit, water, food, twenty-five dollars in quarters, and a hundred one dollar bills. Small denominations and change will come in handy because banking systems and ATMs may be closed or out of order. The amount of items in each bag take into account how many people could be traveling in the car. We also have go bags at our home prepared for each child, ready for them to grab on their way out the door in the event that we're leaving via a different mode of transportation, like on foot or a motorcycle, which brings me to my next point.

What to Do When Driving Your Car Isn't an Option

What happens if the emergency scenario with which your kids are faced doesn't allow for you or them to hop in a car and make a getaway? That's where bicycles and motorcycles come into play. My first and only experience with motorcycles was years before meeting

Ryan, when I rode on the back of a Harley with a suave CIA operations officer who had an uncanny resemblance to Matthew McConaughey. I guess you could say I was living out my very own *How to Lose a Guy in 10 Days* fantasy. That relationship crashed and burned about as quickly as it had heated up, but thankfully, the motorcycle didn't. Nonetheless, zipping through traffic at top speed was frightful enough for me that I didn't plan to get back on one anytime soon, or ever.

My next encounter with motorcycles was entirely different.

"Hold on tight!" I yelled back to six-year-old Lena as she leaned close to me on Ryan's four-wheeler. We were closely trailing him and his two oldest kids, who were leaving us in the dust on their dirt bikes. That's right—Hannah and Hunter, who were nine and eight at the time, were riding their very own Honda 50cc motorcycles ahead of us. Lena, even at six years old, knew how to ride but had chosen to ride with me on the four-wheeler. Now, instead of trying to impress a twentysomething CIA hotshot operations officer with my bravery, I was putting on my brave face for a first grader. I couldn't let on how much I felt out of my element. If she wasn't scared, I certainly couldn't be.

Ryan had taught the Bigs since they were old enough to reach the pegs how to ride motorcycles. He began with balance bikes, then moved to bicycles and then to motorcycles. I never believed him when he told me that Hunter was riding a bike without training wheels at two years old. He didn't have any pictures or video to prove it, and I assumed it was nothing more than a proud parent's exaggeration. It wasn't until Ari took off on his own bike without training wheels at two years old that I knew it had gone exactly the way Ryan had described with Hunter.

Next came motorcycles. Ryan believed then—and still does—that this skill is critical to have in the event that roads become impassable for cars. In just about every apocalyptic or natural disaster movie, there's a scene of people trying to get out of town or somehow get to safety. Roads and freeways are blocked off or traffic is at a standstill. And just like Elijah Wood navigates around gridlocked traffic in the movie *Deep Impact*, we're ready to do the same with our motorcycles. For this reason, we always have enough motorcycles to accommodate our whole family if we ever need to make an escape due to some type of natural disaster or emergency. Bicycles can work in the same way, especially in big cities.

When Ryan worked in downtown Seattle, he even kept an extra motorcycle at his office. He used it to drive to and from different buildings downtown, but the primary reason it was there was in case he needed to get out of the city quickly. For example, Seattle is in a fault zone, and there's often talk of how we're overdue for a massive earthquake, the Big One. We knew that if that were to happen, it would be nearly impossible for Ryan to get out of the city and over Lake Washington to our home near the Cascade Range. Having a motorcycle there gave us all peace of mind that he stood a chance of making it back to us quickly and safely.

While all the Bigs have been riding motorcycles since they were small, what's perhaps most impressive is that Hannah received her motorcycle endorsement just after receiving her driver's license at sixteen years old. She was the only female in her class, and was by far the youngest student. Several grown men didn't pass the test that day, but with years of experience driving motorcycles under her belt, Hannah did it with ease—no doubt surprising many of those men in the process. But if you're still not convinced that you should ride a motorcycle (full disclosure, I'm not entirely there yet, so it's okay if you're not either), or that you should put your kids on them (I'm also still working on this idea with the Littles, TBH), you can consider an alternative, like a scooter, bicycle, or electric bike.

In fact, I find scooters much more palatable than motorcycles, and when we were dating, Ryan brought my dream of riding and owning one to life. Although I had wanted a Vespa for as long as I could remember, it was one of those things I would have never bought for myself. I didn't think I was adventurous enough to own one. After all, I had never even driven one. But I loved the look of them, and even more, I loved picturing myself scooting around some European city on one with a baguette tucked in my backpack. Maybe in another lifetime, I often thought.

"Oh, I love that little red Vespa," I said to Ryan as I pointed to one parked alongside the entrance to Pike Place Market.

"Oh yeah?"

"Yeah, I've always wanted one," I said in passing. I didn't think much of my comment as we walked on to Le Panier, our favorite French bakery. In fact, the conversation didn't even register as memorable to me, or as much of a conversation at all. So you can imagine my surprise when Ryan showed up on my doorstep with a little red Vespa some months later.

"It's yours!" he said with a big smile on his face.

"What do you mean, it's mine?" I asked, flabbergasted.

"I bought it for you! You said you've always wanted one," he said proudly.

I didn't know what to say. To be honest, I was hoping the next big gesture would be a marriage proposal, but I knew Ryan, having just gone through a divorce, was a little gun-shy about moving forward.

And yes, I *had* always wanted a Vespa. The only problem was: I didn't know how to ride one. But soon, with Ryan's help, I learned. And while it wasn't a marriage proposal, it was the perfect kind of grand gesture women swoon over when watching rom-coms. A year later, we hopped on that same Vespa and rode away from our wedding reception, so I guess you can say it all worked out. What I didn't know at the time was how Ryan was already making me more prepared for emergencies well before we became parents together.

Key Principles to Teach Your Kids About Survival

While we recommend finding your own area of interest to dive deep on survival training with your kids, here's a quick wrap-up of what Ryan and I believe are some of the most important techniques and skills to teach your children. Some families may choose to dedicate an entire period of time, say, a day or a week, to teaching their children survival concepts; however, we recommend weaving them into your kids' daily life over time in a more organic way. After all, we want these to be fun concepts that are multipurpose without feeling too intimidating or frightening to our kids. We use the following techniques with our kids, and we recommend you adopt them for your family:

1. Make your own survival kits, and involve your kids in the process. Whether your kids are young and ready for adventure bags or teenagers preparing to get behind the wheel, sit down together at the kitchen table and make their very own, personalized survival bags. Make sure they have an instrumental role in choosing what goes into the bags and that they understand the use for each item. An emergency bag won't do them any good if they don't know what's in there. Ari's adventure bag has now become a staple for every hike, and as an added bonus, it doubles as a key part of his Indiana Jones costume for the next Halloween.

2. Know how to improvise. Make sure your kids know how to improvise for when technology fails, and it *will* fail them at some point or another. In a world of cell phones and Google Maps, kids need to understand the risks of depending on technology to get out of trouble. In an emergency scenario, cell phone networks could be down, and your kids should know how to improvise. For example, on a night when our daughters suspected they were being followed, they ducked into a gas station and asked to use the phone since they had forgotten their cell phones at home. In a perfect world, they wouldn't have forgotten their cell phones that evening, but this isn't a perfect world. We have to remember that these are kids we're talking about, and they won't remember every piece of advice we've given them at all times. They need to know how to think on their feet. Make it a practice to walk your kids through various scenarios to ensure they have an idea of what they would do if things went wrong—they forgot a cell phone, their car broke down, or the road was blocked due to a landslide, for example. If they have an understanding that sometimes things go differently than expected and that they can't always rely on technology, that will help prepare them to come up with alternate plans themselves.

3. Get back to basics. In the event that things don't go as planned and your kids are forced to improvise, knowing how to use a map and compass and understanding north, south, east, and west can be not only useful skills but also lifesaving. They should have a basic awareness of primitive navigation skills, like where the sun rises and sets and how to use the stars to find their way. Harvard physics professor and author of *The Lost Art of Finding Our Way*, John Huth, learned the importance of these abilities firsthand while kayaking off Nantucket Sound. When the fog rolled in, Huth was able to successfully navigate back to safety without a compass because he had paid attention to environmental cues like wind and wave direction prior to leaving the shore. He later learned that two other kayakers weren't so lucky that day and perished in those same conditions.[2] In addition to environmental cues, you can also teach your kids to use landmarks to help orient themselves. For example, once we felt the Bigs were appropriate ages—for us that was fifteen, thirteen, and eleven—we began dropping them off in downtown Seattle to spend summer days navigating the city. We gave them a paper map and told them a meeting location and time to return at the end of the day, and off they went. You want your kids to have this same confidence and ability whether it's getting around a major city, finding their way out of the woods, or getting back to dry land.

4. Designate a family meeting spot. Speaking of meeting locations, we don't only use them for days when we drop our kids off in Seattle. We recommend having a secret family meeting spot so that if you already are or become separated in the event of an emergency like a natural disaster, you can find each other. You should have an option A and an option B. For example, if your preferred meeting location, option A, is your home, what happens if a wildfire is engulfing your home and you can't get there? You need an alternate location, option B, that you will all eventually make it to if and when possible.

5. Establish your getaway vehicles. Once you've helped your kids make their survival kits, trained them on how to navigate, and designated your family meeting spot, it's a great idea to confirm multiple forms of transportation in the event of an emergency. Ensure your teenagers' cars are equipped with their survival kits and that they keep their vehicles filled with at least a half tank of gas at all times. Once your vehicles are prepared, consider your options for alternate transportation like we discussed. Maybe this means purchasing and teaching your kids how to ride motorcycles. Maybe instead you opt for a scooter or electric bike. Find what works for your family and have those necessary precautions in place.

6. Look for opportunities to teach your kids CPR and first aid. Just like the CIA trains its officers in first aid and CPR, you should train your kids. Look for opportunities at your local hospitals and fire stations. For example, our Bigs are all CPR-certified and have taken additional courses on first aid and babysitting certification classes at our local hospital.

After you incorporate these techniques and decide the other survival aspects on which you'd like to dive deep, I recommend you continue to weave them into everyday life with your kids. Together, you and your family can have a well-thought-out, strategic emergency-preparedness plan that keeps you from going to the store during this stage. I want you to be able to sit at home and watch the news while thinking to yourself, "Thank goodness we have a garden," or "Thank goodness we have rice and beans stored in the basement to last us for the next month." I want to take away the fear from your family and instead give you a peace that comes with preparation, and I want you to instill that same peace and mind-set in your children. And don't forget to make it fun.

CHAPTER FIVE

GET OFF THE X

Teaching How to Spot and Avoid Danger

One fall evening a few years ago, Ryan received a call from an unknown number. Like many parents, when our kids are out of the house, we answer calls day or night from unknown numbers in case it's them. And this time it was.

Our oldest told Ryan she'd forgotten her cell phone and was calling from a gas station in town. She and her sister had been walking the half-mile trek home and noticed two creepy men on foot following them for several blocks and turns. Rather than continuing to walk in the same direction toward the house, the girls chose an alternate, better-lit route to ensure the men didn't know where they lived. They entered a well-populated gas station, where they asked to borrow the attendant's phone to call us for a ride home.

I happened to be down the street having dinner with some girlfriends in town that night, so Ryan called and asked me to swing by the gas station to pick up the girls. When I arrived, I didn't even see them inside. They had strategically positioned themselves so that they could see out but the men couldn't easily see them.

We got into the car together and drove the short distance back to the house. The girls were a little rattled but otherwise fine. At that point, I didn't think much about the "why" behind what had transpired; I was just happy our daughters were safe. But as I mulled the situation later, I realized that they had actually made some smart, strategic choices in that situation—and it was largely due to the training Ryan had instilled in them since even before they were old enough to walk around the neighborhood on their own.

Get Off the X

One of the tenets of CIA training for the field is the concept of "getting off the X." What is the X? The X equals danger, and it can come in many forms. The X can be anything: a person, a car, a building, an environment—literally any situation in which danger rears its ugly head and your gut tells you to run. It's about identifying danger and acting on it as quickly as possible. The bottom line is you want to get as far away from the X as you can. The longer you stay on the X, the more likely it is that you'll be harmed.

I learned this lesson early in my career at the CIA while preparing for my first temporary duty assignment to sub-Saharan Africa. Though I was largely based at CIA Headquarters in Langley, Virginia, I occasionally did travel abroad to gain on-the-ground observations to deepen my expertise. Upon arrival at our CIA station, I was told that when driving at night, I should consider all traffic lights and stop signs to be an X and not to stop. Instead, I should cautiously roll through them. Smash-and-grabs, in which someone smashes your car window to grab your purse from the passenger's seat, were common there. By stopping for traffic lights in that city, you would make yourself a target for thieves. (It's worth noting that this is *not* a practice I endorse while driving stateside!)

Given the locations to which I traveled, often alone, I was accustomed to being on high alert, ready to get off the X if need be. I stashed money and credit cards under my clothes, and I was ready to give up my wallet or purse on the spot to any thief who wanted it. No amount of money was worth your life, and CIA training taught us to get off the X as quickly as possible—which may mean handing the thief your purse, or if possible, throwing it to the side for them to grab while you ran in the opposite direction.

Although this concept was familiar to me, it wasn't until I met Ryan that I considered teaching "get off the X" to children. My high-security-alert mind-set was a thing I turned on when I traveled to Africa, but when I returned to Northern Virginia, I allowed myself to let down my guard. Ryan turned that view upside down when he told me that he had been teaching the kids to get off the X since as early as they could understand it.

"Aren't they a little young to be thinking about such scary concepts?" I asked him toward the beginning of our relationship. They were six, eight, and ten years old at the time.

"It's only scary to them if you make it scary," he told me. "Teaching them about danger and how to avoid it can actually do the opposite of scaring them. It can empower them."

Ryan's belief was that kids were never too young to start learning these concepts. I worried that by introducing these topics we were essentially stealing away years of their childlike innocence. Can't we let kids be kids for as long as possible? The world can be such a scary place—shouldn't we shield them from it for as long as possible? The reality, however, is that when we take that approach, we're actually doing our kids a disservice. We're not preparing them for the real world. Because one day, they will be out there in the world, and we don't want them just to survive—although that's key, of course—we want them to thrive! And like Ryan explained, when it's done in an age-appropriate way, we're empowering them rather than frightening them. He showed me that our training and fieldwork could be adapted in a different way for us to use in parenting. Moreover, our different experiences—him working as an operations officer in Europe and the Middle East and me as an analyst traveling back and forth to Africa—gave us unique perspectives to teach our children this concept.

And it wasn't just the *idea* of applying this concept to parenting; it was the *way* in which Ryan introduced it to the kids. He had an ability to explain it to them calmly and even make it fun, without creating anxiety or fear. For example, one of my favorite ways was when we drove home to my rental house on the outskirts of town when we were dating. There was a place where the road split into two, and as we neared the fork, Ryan would say, "Oh no, guys! There's someone following us! Should we lose him?" The kids would all excitedly yell, "Yes! Let's *go*!" It was something he did regularly, so they knew what was coming next. Ryan would speed up and at the last second, he'd quickly veer to the right so that we'd be on the frontage road, leaving the imaginary surveillant in the dust.

"Phew! We lost him!" he'd say as he looked over at me and winked.

"Woo-hoo!" the three kids would yell from the backseat.

Now, in reality, CIA training never teaches you to evade someone who is following you (I'll discuss this more in the next chapter), but this was a way that Ryan simplified "get off the X" for the kids to understand at their young ages—that is, there was danger behind us, and we needed to get away from it as quickly as possible.

What's the X in Your Life?

Over the past several years parenting with Ryan, I've learned that in our day-to-day life with the kids, the X can pop up in many different forms, some scarier than others. Does your child want to go to a party hosted by a less-than-trustworthy classmate? That's a potential X, and you might choose for them to skip that one. Or let's say your child has to wait for you to pick them up after soccer practice. Should they start walking home if you're running late and have you pick them up on the side of the road or should they wait at the school? As I learned from my training (and from Ryan), it's not so much get off the X as it is avoid the X altogether.

It can be easy for parents to overanalyze this advice and see the X everywhere. Like I mentioned earlier, this was me for the majority of the first two years of Ari's life. I sometimes skipped events if there were large crowds, and after Gigi was born, I was so intimidated by the thought of taking two kids to the park that I stopped going to some that felt overwhelming to me. At one point, I even put a GPS tracker under Ari's clothes anytime we left the house because I was in constant fear that someone would take him. I also know some moms who don't let their kids go to the movie theater because they're afraid of shootings. What we need to remember, however, is that parks and movie theaters are places to have fun, not places that should foster fear and paranoia in you or your kids. It's all about balance. As years have passed, my anxiety has decreased, in part due to hormones leveling out, but also because Ryan has helped me understand what warrants worrying and how to prepare our children for the world. I was thankful for this preparation when I was at the park with Ari and Gigi one afternoon in the spring just before Gigi turned two years old.

The three of us were halfway around the track, the kids on their bikes and me on foot, when a jogger came up behind us. We pulled over to the side to let him pass, and I noticed he stopped ahead of us to talk with a man on a bike. Both of them seemed out of place at the park—they were dressed in oversize hoodies with the hoods over their heads, casting shadows over much of their faces. The man on foot went the other direction, while the man on the bike passed us and doubled back to circle and pass us again. My gut told me that something was wrong. I tried my best to keep calm and told Ari to hang back and stay closer to me than usual. I knew we needed to make our way to the car, but I tried to keep my cool with the kids in hopes of keeping them calm and getting them to follow instructions.

I scanned my surroundings and quickly went through the options in my head. There were plenty of people at the park that day, but as I looked around, I realized that the distance between everyone else and me was too far for anyone to help if someone took one or both of my kids. And to increase my anxiety even more, we were on a part of the track that was parallel to a main road. If someone took them, they'd be gone before I could do anything about it. I realized that I'd forgotten my pocketknife at home and left my pepper spray in the car—I always tried to carry some type of equalizer on me (more on this in chapter 7)—so I didn't have anything to protect myself or the kids if we were attacked. But what would I be attacked for in broad daylight? I wasn't carrying a purse or any type of bag, so it seemed to me that the only things I had worth taking were my kids themselves. I considered yelling at the man and telling him to stop circling us, but every part of my gut told me not to confront him and to instead calmly get to the car. I also didn't take time to get out my cell phone to snap a photo; instead, I relied on my own eyes to process the GRAB (gender, race, age, and build) of the man so that I could give a description to the police, if necessary. This is a technique I learned at the CIA that I'll talk more about in the next chapter.

By the fourth time the man circled us, I didn't waste any more time. I scooped Gigi off her balance bike and carried both her and the bike the remainder of the way to the car. I told Ari we needed to get to the car as quickly as possible, and when I sensed he was on the verge of a meltdown because he wasn't ready to leave the park (three-year-olds need much more warning to leave the park than this), I promised him a special treat in the car. I knew I had to get them safely to the car, and I couldn't afford any sort of tantrum that could delay us. Once we got to the car, I put the kids in without buckling them and got in and locked the doors. I crawled into the backseat and buckled them in with all of us safely locked inside, rather than my usual routine of buckling them while leaning in from the parking lot.

I lost sight of the man on the bike, and as I safely drove away from the park, I went over the events in my mind. I breathed deeply and told myself, *They're safe. We're safe. We're okay.* When I saw those two men talking to each other, something in my gut told me that they were working in tandem, and despite my efforts, I couldn't shake the feeling that I had almost lost my kids. It wasn't enough to make me call the police, though, because after all, nothing had actually happened, right? Why would I distract them from actual police business? It wasn't until a phone call with my mom an hour later that I realized I needed to call.

"You should call the police right away and let them know," she said. "You don't want something to happen to someone else. Think about all of the other moms that go there with their kids."

"Yeah, you're right. I should let them know. I don't want this to happen to someone else and, God forbid, have a different outcome." I immediately hung up and dialed the police department's nonemergency line.

The dispatcher answered, and I explained in detail what had happened at the park.

"I worked at the CIA for years, and I've been trained in surveillance-detection techniques." I didn't usually throw around my prior CIA experience in conversations (it caused an instant eye roll for me whenever I heard anyone do this), but this time I did, because I feared I wouldn't be taken seriously. What if they thought I was just some overreacting mom?

"I'm not just a mom who's overreacting," I continued. "This is the most scared I've ever felt somewhere with my kids. Something was wrong, and I know it."

I repeated the same line, attempting to justify my bona fides, to the police officer who called me ten minutes later. I soon learned that I didn't need to justify anything because my instincts had been right.

"I wish you had called sooner," the officer said.

"Oh?"

"I was just at the park and made contact with the individual because we had multiple calls about him. When I stopped at the park, I found him in the bathroom doing drugs."

The officer explained that if something like this happened again I should call right away. I said I would but noted that I hoped it wouldn't.

I hung up the phone and cried as I sat on the edge of my bed, processing everything I had just learned. While the police officer didn't confirm to me that this was a potential kidnapper, learning that the man was on drugs explained his erratic behavior and told me that my gut was right that something was off with this encounter. It was one of those situations when you don't really want to be right. You hope that maybe you actually *were* the overreacting mother. I was still shaken up when Ryan got home from work a few hours later.

"You did everything right," he assured me. "You got off the X."

"Yeah, I guess you're right," I said. "But I should have called the police sooner. I can't stop thinking how close I was to losing our babies," I said as I collapsed into his arms, tears streaming down my face again. There were so many months after each of the Littles was born when I was paralyzed by the fear that someone could take my kids, and now I had faced that fear head-on. I know the anxiety won't ever go away entirely for me, but being prepared to identify and avoid dangerous situations helped me get through *this* situation, and it continues to help me live more confidently day-to-day with my kids.

Key Principles to Teach Your Kids to Spot and Avoid Danger

I don't just want these techniques to help *you* feel prepared to get off the X; I want you to teach these techniques to your kids, which will in turn give you even more peace of mind over time. In order to do this, you'll need to remember that it's a balancing act. We need to let our kids be kids while also giving them a level of smart independence. We can do that by teaching them some key principles to help them spot their own X's so that they can hopefully avoid them entirely, or if not, be prepared to react in the safest way.

1. Listen to your gut. One of the most important lessons you can teach your kids is how to spot danger, and so much of that has to do with listening to their spidey sense. Teach your kids to tune in to the feeling they get when the hairs on the back of their necks stand up— this can be a useful barometer for when they should utilize the following practices and get off the X. Ryan learned this the hard way when he first began his CIA operational training.

-RYAN-

TRUST YOUR GUT

I learned to get off the X early in my CIA career. In fact, it's one of my first memories at the CIA's covert spy-training facility known as the Farm. We were learning about how to operate in high-threat environments where roadside bombs and different types of terrorist attacks are prevalent. One night during an exercise, I was driving down a dark road with three of my classmates and an instructor. I knew I'd be embarrassed if I made a mistake. What I didn't know at the time was that one of the best ways to learn in CIA training—and to have it burned on my brain—was to fail. In fact, most exercises were designed to make at least some of the students fail. Those students became the class example the next day as the instructors walked through lessons learned to ensure no one would ever make that same mistake in real life, when the stakes were much higher.

As we drove down the road, our doors locked and eyes peeled, not knowing what obstacle we'd face, we spotted something about a hundred yards ahead of us. Perhaps it was a box or garbage; we couldn't tell, but we knew it looked a little suspicious. It was then that I noticed headlights from an approaching car in my rearview mirror. Was the threat ahead of us or behind us, or both? Or were they false alarms? The ability to make quick, logical judgments was a trait CIA officers were expected to have in the real world, and we had the opportunity to demonstrate this ability around the clock during these several months of intense operational training. Rather than speed past the unidentified object in front of us, our group chose to drive slowly toward the box to ascertain whether it was indeed the threat or if the threat came from the looming headlights behind us. The next thing I knew, the instructor leaned over my shoulder and said, "You're all dead." A figurative roadside bomb had just killed us; we had gotten too close to the X.

I remember thinking to myself that I knew I should have turned the car around, but for some reason I felt the need to validate the threat first. Did I know it was a roadside bomb? No. Did I know it could be one? Yes. And that's why I should have driven in the opposite direction. I soon learned that the majority of students reacted to this training scenario in the same way I did. Despite having just learned about getting off the X the day before in the classroom, I ignored the hairs on the back of my neck telling me to drive away and chose instead to drive closer to the package.

Most of the trainees during this introduction get too close to the box, and when it explodes, they "die." It's a difficult lesson to learn right off the bat at the Farm. Trust your gut. If something looks suspicious, it is.

There are several different ways you can begin to teach your kids how to listen to their gut. Talk to them about a specific experience that they had and how it made them feel. For our kids, it was the girls' experience of feeling like they were being followed. If your kids haven't had a firsthand experience of something that just doesn't feel quite right, you can use several different types of examples to help illustrate the point.

Picture this: Your daughter is out at a restaurant with her friend and her friend's parents. They enjoy a delicious dinner, and the parents have wine with their meal—not something terribly out of the ordinary. However, your daughter notices that her friend's dad has several glasses and is starting to act funny. He's much more boisterous than his normal, quiet self, and when he gets up to use the restroom, he stumbles a bit. Your daughter starts to feel a little sick to her stomach because she knows he's the one who is supposed to drive her home. What should she do?

This is a great illustration to discuss with your kids not only what it feels like to listen to their gut but also appropriate ways to get out of a situation like this, which is another version of getting off the X. In this story, we would recommend to our kids that they say they're not feeling well and ask to call us so that we can come pick them up. That will then inevitably lead to a conversation that you'll need to have with your partner about boundaries and whether that's a home you want your daughter to go to again or if you'd like to discuss the event in detail with the parents yourselves. The most important takeaway from this story, though, is for your child to act on their gut and get off the X, even if that means in the end that they ultimately offend someone—that's okay.

We've found, however, that with some of our kids, it's useful to have built-in excuses because they're more sensitive to other people's feelings and hesitant to speak up directly for fear of offending someone. If you know that's your child too, then prepare them beforehand with the ways that they could get out of a situation like this. This is also a great opportunity to ensure you have some type of code word with your child that they can either say on the phone or text you if they're in a situation in which their gut tells them they need to leave, with no questions asked. You have an agreement that when they invoke this code word, you will come pick them up or give them an excuse to leave while allowing them to save face.

You can also talk to your kids about listening to their gut through examples from a show or movie that your child likes. The movie *Finding Nemo* demonstrates this point perfectly when Dory wants to swim through the trench because something tells her that it's safer, but she doesn't know exactly what. Marlin, however, insists that they swim over the trench, which results in them swimming through stinging jellyfish. Like Dory, your kids may also not be able to explain *why* they feel like they should or shouldn't do something, but helping them to understand that it's okay—and even good—to act on that inner voice is what we want to do. (Of course, in Dory's case it was because someone had told her not to swim over it, but she just couldn't remember due to her short-term memory loss.) If Marlin and Dory had listened to Dory's gut, they would have easily and safely made it through the trench.

If your kids are older and you feel comfortable with them watching the movie *Taken* with Liam Neeson, pay attention to the scene where Amanda and Kim share a cab with Peter from the airport. Notice Kim's face when Amanda agrees to share the cab with him. Her eyes shift from Peter to Amanda and back to Peter. That right there is Kim's gut telling her that this isn't a good idea. When they arrive at the apartment and Amanda tells him they're staying there alone—again, not a good idea—and then agrees to go to a party with him, Kim verbalizes her gut feeling when she says to Amanda, "We don't even know him!" To which Amanda responds, "What's not to know? He's hot," immediately shutting down Kim's intuition. This movie is an extreme dramatization of the type of danger your kids could encounter, and one that I don't think you should lie awake worrying about at night; I share it, however, because it is a clear example of what listening to your gut can look like, and it can make it easier for your kids to understand.

2. Visualize your escape route. When emergencies happen, it can become chaotic quickly, and it's common for people to become "frozen." It's important to register what's happening as quickly as possible so that you can keep moving as opposed to freezing in place as events unfold around you.

-RYAN-

WHEN I FROZE AT THE FARM

I learned the importance of not freezing in an emergency scenario when I encountered a training ambush at the Farm. In a well-planned ambush, the targets won't survive unless they find a way to get off the X quickly. I experienced this in an exercise when my convoy was told to meet some individuals at a predetermined location. As my colleagues and I exited our vehicles in the open ravine, we found ourselves pinned down by instructors who had set up in the elevated tree line. They had high ground and superior firepower. We were equipped with small paintball pistols, but we stood no chance against their higher-powered paintball rifles.

As I leaned up against the side of my car, paintballs whizzed at us from seemingly all directions. I felt the force of the impact of them hitting the edge of the car and felt fragments from the ones hitting my classmates. Paint exploding everywhere, I was frozen, not knowing what to do for several seconds. Instead of getting off the X, I found myself raising my paintball gun in the air with one arm, shooting over the roof of the car without seeing my targets. As we continued to stay on this X, more and more of us were "killed."

The five or so trainees who got off the X as soon as the ambush began survived. In this high-adrenaline situation, however, the remaining fifteen of us forgot our training. We resorted to gross motor skills and clumsy movements. We threw all of our training out the window, and just about all of us began returning fire. Staying to fight back from our weakened positions led to our "deaths."

Visualizing how you would react in potential "get off the X" situations beforehand and mentally preparing for how you would keep moving can make all the difference. For example, where are your go-to places that you visit each day? Do you have a regular coffee stop each morning? If something happened at that location, how would you get off the X? When going to a movie, restaurant, or sporting event, do you know where the exits are? Would you have a plan for exiting as quickly as possible if necessary?

Once you've incorporated this into *your* daily routine, you can teach your kids the same technique. You can game-plan scenarios with them to discuss what they would do. We often do this with our kids as it relates to sports, dance, theater, and other extracurricular hobbies. This strategy has been most helpful with Lena and sports. She takes feedback extraordinarily well and almost always adjusts her playing to reflect the changes Ryan has gone over with her.

"I want you to picture yourself dribbling down the field," Ryan would tell Lena. This had become a ritual before all of her soccer games.

"Okay, got it."

"No, really. Close your eyes. Do you see it?" This sometimes prompted an eye roll or two, but Ryan would soldier on. "I want you to see yourself dribbling the ball down the field. . . . Picture yourself weaving around the defenders, using their momentum against them to cut in the opposite direction. And don't kick the ball to the goalie—drive it all the way and kick it in the corner."

We tell our kids to mentally prepare and visualize scoring the winning soccer goal, driving to the basketball hoop for the game-winning shot, or nailing the most difficult part of their dance routine in their minds before actually doing it. They need to visualize themselves succeeding ahead of time to help them make the right choices when it's game time. In short, what you visualize and do in practice is what you'll do in the game.

In a security context, you can teach your kids to look for exits when they enter a room so they're prepared to get off the X. For instance, when you arrive at a movie theater or restaurant and they've had time to settle in their seats, ask them to close their eyes and tell you the number of exits and where they are. My dad did this with me when I was growing up, and it remains something I do to this day for myself and for the kids. It sounds extreme, but only if you make it so.

3. Listen to alarms and warning signals. In addition to visualization techniques, I also recommend emphasizing to your kids the importance of listening and acting quickly when there is an alarm telling them to leave a building or location. They shouldn't assume it's a drill. Researchers from the Universities of Greenwich, Ulster, and Liverpool conducted a study on the survivors of the 9/11 attacks and found that 90 percent of the survivors delayed their evacuation from the World Trade Center buildings, sometimes by nearly a half hour, to do things like save their work or shut down their computers.[1]

"We need to train people that when you hear the alarm, you need to get out. It is not important to shut down the computer or save documents," Professor Ed Galea, project director at the University of Greenwich, said.

I couldn't agree more. Sometimes, however, people are hesitant to react to an alarm because they assume it's a drill. They look around to see how others are responding. They take time to ask what's going on. They change their shoes. They go to the restroom. But what's the worst thing that can happen if it turns out to be a false alarm? Would you be embarrassed that you were the only one who darted out the door? Maybe. But that doesn't compare to the possible harmful outcome if you wait around to see if others are evacuating before deciding what you should do for yourself.

I recommend teaching your kids to respond to all alarms (drills or not) with a sense of urgency and purpose while maintaining their calmness to the extent possible. The more you have these types of discussions with your kids, the more prepared they'll be if they encounter this kind of scenario. And this is a big *if*. Ryan and I like to approach emergency scenarios with our kids in the same way the CIA approaches training. We recommend you discuss and prepare them for worst-case scenarios so that they're ready, all the while knowing that nearly everything they encounter in real life won't be as difficult.

4. Run, hide, fight. If a CIA officer has to pull out a weapon, she's done something wrong. In fact, fighting is the last thing you want to do if you find yourself in a dangerous scenario. The first choice is always to get off the X if at all possible, followed by hiding and, as a last resort, fighting.

This concept is often introduced as "run, hide, fight," and Ryan has taught it as part of active-shooter training in his security work in his various roles in the private sector. He believes this basic idea can also be taught in training scenarios in school settings and is a concept our kids should understand. For example, in a shooting or violent attack, the first thing your kids should do is run (i.e., get off the X). It's important that you and your kids don't confuse getting off the X with fight-or-flight. This isn't about running away from danger in a cowardly way. It's about teaching your children to get themselves out of a potentially dangerous spot. If your kids are unable to run, then they should hide. If they're unable to run or hide, then the last resort is to fight the attacker. This preference order isn't necessarily intuitive for kids or even adults. In some emergency situations, people can feel a false sense of security when hiding, or they may simply be too scared to move. But we emphasize with our kids that running, if possible, should be their first option, because running is the only thing that will take you away from danger. If you have to hide or fight, that means you're staying on the X, and this is the last place you should be. That being said, if hiding and fighting are your only options, then you hide as if your life depended on it, and you fight like a badass (I'll get to what fighting like a badass means for security-conscious parents in chapter 7).

5. Ignore authority figures, if necessary. Surprisingly, sometimes getting off the X may actually be the opposite of what you're instructed to do—which brings us to the next lesson for your children. There are times when it's not only appropriate but also critical to ignore orders from authority figures. You may be familiar with the sinking of the Japanese-built South Korean ferry known as the Sewol ferry disaster. On the morning of April 16, 2014, the ferry sank and 304 of the total 476 passengers and crew aboard the boat perished. Many of those who died were secondary school students. News media reported that as the ship sank, a voice over the intercom told passengers not to move because it was dangerous. Given that many were children, they were likely frightened and inclined to follow orders. Some of those who jumped or ran to the top of the ship were rescued. Those who stayed as the voice over the intercom instructed did not survive.[2]

Yes, it's about getting off the X, but it's about more than that. Something Ryan and I learned time and time again at the CIA, which I'll discuss throughout this book, is the importance of thinking critically. It's good to ask questions, even of authority figures. We recommend teaching your children that there's a time to do what's asked of you, but if it doesn't seem right, then push back—respectfully, of course.

It's extremely important for our kids to know that just because someone is an adult doesn't mean that person is always right. As your children become older, they must learn to think critically for themselves and to question authority. If they already have some critical-thinking skills and a foundational understanding of the need to sometimes question authority, they'll be more inclined to think for themselves in an emergency scenario. We recognize, of course, that cultures have different social norms with regard to established hierarchies, and that may have been a factor at play in the Sewol ferry disaster. Our perspective on this issue—and others—is heavily Western-focused, and we understand questioning authority figures may be even more uncomfortable for those who come from cultures that place significant value on respecting and listening to elders.

In addition to discussing what it means to get off the X and encouraging your children to think critically, we emphasize to our kids that in an emergency scenario, they won't be in trouble with us for following their gut and putting these principles into practice. For example, say there is an emergency at school, and they're told to stay put or face disciplinary consequences like detention. Their gut, however, tells them to leave. In a situation like this, our kids know that we'll always have their backs. That doesn't necessarily mean they won't have to face consequences for their actions at school, but *we* won't punish them for getting off the X as we've taught them to do. We'll also advocate for and defend them to the school's leadership team, if necessary. Knowing that we'll always have their backs gives them the confidence to think critically for themselves and make their own choices in an emergency scenario, even if that means going against an authority figure.

I've given you a lot of information, and some of it might feel intimidating or even make you a little anxious. That's okay—it's normal to feel that way. But I want you to know that you don't need to be para-noid or worried all the time. That's not the takeaway here. Instead, I want you to equip your kids with the skills to think critically so that if they ever find themselves in a dangerous situation, their chance of survival increases. Better yet, these techniques will ideally help them make proactive, commonsense decisions that allow them to identify and avoid danger altogether. We'll never know if those men following close behind our daughters that night truly had bad inten-tions or if it was simply an act of abundant caution on our daughters' part. That being said, anytime they listen to their intuition and get off the X, Ryan and I consider that to be good practice of the tech-niques we seek to solidify in their approach to life. Likewise, as your kids are running out your front door and into the world, I want you to be able to say to them, "Hey, remember to get off the X if you need to," and for them to know exactly what you mean.

CHAPTER SIX

LOOK WITHOUT LOOKING

How to Be Aware of Your Surroundings

Our son Ari had just turned two years old when he went with Ryan to the car dealership for a routine oil change. Ryan was paying the cashier when Ari suddenly burst into tears and pointed out the window. That's when Ryan saw a man get into a black Cadillac Escalade and start to drive off. He quickly realized that Ari thought the black Escalade was our black Chevy Suburban.

"Did you think someone was driving away in our car?" he asked Ari.

"Yes!" he managed to yell out through his tears.

"That's not our car, Ari. Ours is over there," Ryan said as he pointed across the street to where the attendant had left our Suburban.

"Oh," Ari said with a look of confusion and then relief.

It was this situation that taught us that it's never too early to teach our children how to be aware of their surroundings. Part of this awareness includes recognizing makes and models of vehicles, something Ryan and I learned in-depth at the CIA, and Ari was proving that he was already ahead of the game. Once kids can do this and master other basic concepts like directional awareness, you'll find that they have a stronger ability to see more of what's going on around them. As your kids get older, you can incorporate the more sophisticated surveillance-detection principles and security-awareness techniques that Ryan and I learned in our CIA training and used on a day-to-day basis in our intelligence operations.

The Twists and Turns of Surveillance Detection

"I made the wrong call," I managed to get out through my sobbing.

"Oh no, sweetie. I'm so sorry," Ryan attempted to console me through the phone. We were only a few weeks into our dating relationship, but I knew he was the only person I could call who would really understand what I was going through. Not only had he completed basic surveillance-detection training like the course I was currently enrolled in, he had also graduated from advanced surveillance-detection training, which was even more complex and demanding. He knew exactly what I was dealing with . . . and he could appreciate just how I'd screwed up.

If only Ryan could actually comfort me in person. But he couldn't. Instead, I sat in my government-owned vehicle on the side of a dark street in Northern Virginia with tears streaming down my face, while he was all the way back home.

"My route wasn't good . . . I second-guessed myself . . . I thought I had a surveillance team on me, but I just wasn't seeing them. I only have one more exercise tomorrow, and if I fail that one I won't get certified," I told Ryan as I tried to stop crying.

"You won't fail tomorrow. You haven't failed any other run. To-night was a mistake, and you'll be back on your game tomorrow," he assured me.

Ryan was right. I nailed my surveillance training exercise the following afternoon, but it wasn't before a return to the classroom in the morning, where my failure to make the right call—that is, whether or not someone was following me—made me one of the class examples of what *not* to do. What I didn't know before this course was that the DO depended on several students making the wrong call during the exercise so that they could use these students' mistakes as learning opportunities for the whole class. This time, I was one of those students. This approach to training guaranteed that the students would never make that mistake again. It can also be mirrored in parenting if done appropriately, and it's something I'll revisit later in the book.

A surveillance-detection route is what the CIA calls a preplanned circuitous route that enables an individual to determine whether they're being followed. It was one of the lengthier portions of train-ing for CIA operations officers down at the Farm; instructors de-voted several months to teaching the art of surveillance and then gave plenty of time for operations officers to practice their newly learned skills throughout the remaining months of training. It was rare for analysts like me to have the training, but my rotational as-signment in the DO required an intensive, at times grueling surveillance-detection course. It was there that I learned how to plan a route with natural look-backs, how to identify makes and models of cars by their headlights in the dark, and ultimately how to ensure I was arriving at my asset meeting clandestinely to ensure their safety and my own.

While in this training, I learned that the key to surveillance detection in intelligence operations is to look natural and never let on that you know when you're being followed. Unlike in the movies, when you often see a chase develop and spies try to lose their tail, this sort of showboating getaway is the *last* thing you'd want to do in real life. Instead of dramatically racing through city streets, the true art of surveillance detection involves developing a route that makes you look like a normal person going about your everyday life—running errands or visiting tourist destinations, for example. If you're successful at this, any intelligence team that's following you will likely decide you're not worth their time or resources, and they'll move on to another target—making you free to conduct your operations another day.

In order to know whether you're being followed, you need to confirm your surveillance with multiple sightings over time, distance, and change in direction. These factors are necessary because they take into account coincidence. You may see the same person at the grocery store and then again at the post office, but that doesn't necessarily mean they're following you. That person may also need to stop at those two locations. If you see that person at 9:00 a.m. at the grocery store, again an hour later at a restaurant across town, and then for a third time when you're picking up your dry cleaning—that's a confirmed sighting. In order to confirm sightings, it's important to learn how to memorize a physical description of the people you see on foot. If you're in a vehicle, it's necessary to memorize makes and models of vehicles you see in your rearview mirror as well as read license plate numbers backward, all while not looking suspicious.

Although I had worked at the CIA for several years by the time I took this surveillance course, these skills were entirely new to me. Indeed, my work up to that point had been heavily focused on researching and analyzing African politics; the only memorizing I was doing was of the various ethnic groups in the region, certainly not license plates. I had even traveled internationally as an undercover CIA analyst countless times, but those posts hadn't involved fieldwork like this. After becoming certified in surveillance detection, I started preparing for my next trip to East Africa a few months later. I knew this time it would be different. This time, I would see things I had never noticed before.

I was only a few days into my trip when I had the distinct feeling I was being followed as I meandered through the dusty, narrow stalls of the market—each one filled with intricately carved wooden safari animals, the perfect souvenir for Western tourists. I glanced over at the wood carvers who sat under a baobab tree outside the market, smoking cigarettes and drinking bottles of orange Fanta before making their next batch of carvings. There was little differentiating the market stalls from one another, making the owners all the more eager to draw me into their store to make the sale.

"Hello, sister! You are welcome. Come in!" they all pleaded with me in their thick East African accents.

On some trips to the region, I responded in their native Swahili, telling them I was not a tourist and wouldn't settle for their inflated prices. They were surprised to hear the words flow so easily from my mouth, and it almost always guaranteed a lower price. While I had learned Swahili in college in Indiana, I'd perfected it as a student in northern Tanzania. I was fascinated with the language from day one—the melodic sound, the structure, the culture. Day after day, I found myself engrossed in Swahili and African politics. I couldn't wait to finish my degree so I could begin a career I was certain would take me back to Africa, and here I was just a few years later, one of the CIA's only Swahili-speaking spies, navigating dirt roads in the same region I had spent time in as a naive college junior.

On this particular trip, I chose not to advertise my knowledge of the language due to the sensitive nature of the operations I was conducting. I soon learned this worked to my advantage.

As I was looking at bags, I noticed a local woman, hands covered in henna, enter the store.

"She's looking at the bags now," she said in Swahili into her old-school Nokia cell phone. She closely watched me browse the store, careful to keep several feet of distance between us, all the while completely unaware I understood her every word.

I was being followed.

Intense CIA operational training had prepared me for moments like this, although I'd never expected it would be as easy as overhearing someone give a play-by-play of my every move. As I crossed the street, I also noticed a tall slender man wearing the same dusty, once-white Adidas tennis shoes that I had seen earlier in the day at a different market on the other side of town. I knew from my training that while surveillants often changed their clothes when following a target, they rarely changed shoes, which sometimes made it easier to spot them. I chuckled to myself that morning in the market. It was true I was on a mission, but not the clandestine kind the host country intelligence service hoped they would catch me conducting. That day I was focused on finding souvenirs to bring back home for Ryan and the kids, so I went about my business, knowing that while they were wasting their time watching me, one of my colleagues was out conducting actual espionage right under their noses.

-RYAN-

CATCHING THEM IN THE ACT

When you get really good at detecting surveillance, you find that you can spot it even when you're not the target of the surveillance team. For example, when I was in France attending a family wedding, my extended family was gathering in the town square of a small city outside Paris. I was standing and observing the environment around me as we were waiting for everyone to arrive when I noticed a man walking toward a store on the far side of the square. Much to my surprise, I began to notice multiple members of a surveillance team spread out in their various positions, working together to follow their target.

I couldn't believe it. In my career up until this point, I had never had a legitimate foreign surveillance team follow me while conducting an operation, perhaps a true testament to my ability to conduct non-alerting clandestine operations. Yet here I was, on vacation, witnessing a foreign surveillance team in action. I watched the team shift positions and set up strategically while the man was in the store. When he eventually exited, I continued to observe the surveillance team members fall into place as they followed their target to his next location. What was more surprising than anything was that while I watched this all take place right in front of my eyes, no one else had a clue what was going on around them! Granted, I had been trained in surveillance and countersurveillance, but the reality is that if you train yourself to be aware of your surroundings, you never know what you'll start to see.

Observing Your Own Environment

So how does all this seemingly unique surveillance-detection training translate to parenting? Teaching your kids to sharpen their observation skills through surveillance detection can increase their general security awareness and, as a result, their safety. This skill can be practiced as a passenger in a car, train, or bus, and even on foot, so kids can be taught before they're old enough to drive. In fact, we've found that these techniques can be helpful even for our youngest children. Within months of the story I shared of Ari at the car dealership, he could spot nearly ten makes and models on the road at any given time.

You never know when a skill like this will become useful. Even if it's not until adulthood, you've already given your kids a head start. If your toddler isn't interested in memorizing makes and models of cars, don't be alarmed. And by no means should you get out the flash cards. This is something that can and should happen organically through pointing them out on the road. With Ari, we started by teaching him the names of our own vehicles. Spotting "Daddy's car" on the road became a fun game for me to play with him when we were out and about, and from there, I began pointing out other makes and models. You can also begin teaching these skills through games like slug bug, in which you call out every time you see a Volkswagen Beetle (it's usually accompanied by a punch, but I'll leave that part to your discretion!), or pediddle, a game at night when you point out the cars with one headlight. To make it more interesting, you can guess the car based on the one remaining headlight. This skill set is most age-appropriate for your preteens and teens—I simply offer the illustration of Ari as an example of early exposure and to explain how I'm beginning to implement some of these parenting techniques with the Littles.

As you can imagine, these skills become even more applicable when your kids start driving. We began discussing these topics with our kids well before any of them got behind the wheel, and when our oldest, Hannah, started driving, none of the topics we were introducing to her were new; however, they took on new meaning as she began experiencing them firsthand.

In order for anyone, especially teenage drivers, to have an awareness of what's happening around them on the road, they need to have a high level of comfort and confidence when they're behind the wheel. The idea behind this is that the more comfortable they feel driving a car, the more they can rely on their senses to look around them and notice anything that's off. When Hannah and Hunter each received their learner's driving permits, Ryan used the same approach to teach them how to drive. The very first time he took them driving, he directed them to the on-ramp for the interstate. This seemed extreme to me—I remembered waiting weeks or even longer before my driver's education teacher allowed me to merge onto the interstate for the first time.

Ryan, however, insisted that this was critical to building their confidence while driving and to begin teaching them the importance of hand, eye, and foot coordination in a vehicle. As the kids drove onto the on-ramp, he told them to floor the gas until they reached seventy-five miles per hour. He then told them to turn and look over their shoulder as they merged onto the freeway, all while keeping the car driving straight between the lines. This ability to handle the car while speeding up and looking behind them is an excellent initial building block for increasing that confidence and security awareness.

Ryan's approach to teaching the kids how to drive is less conservative than that of other driving instructors, but there's a reason for this. One of the most important driving exercises in his time at the Farm was when he drove an obstacle and speed course *in reverse*, an exercise he later adapted for the Bigs. Many of the students struggled with this exercise, whereas Ryan, who once drove a one-way five-mile-long loop entirely in reverse as a sixteen-year-old boy wanting to impress a girl, excelled. I'm not sure who I've heard say "I'm the world's best backwards driver" more—Ryan or Mater from Disney's *Cars*. I do know that he had the fastest times in all the driving courses in his Farm class, even rivaling those of the best instructors.

After Hannah and Hunter had conquered their first experience merging onto the interstate, Ryan took them to an empty parking lot, where they practiced driving backward for nearly two hours. The logic behind this training was that if you could drive your car in reverse, then you could drive it forward even better. It was another example of how the CIA made every training situation more difficult than real life. I wasn't in the car for either of these first-time exercises—I stayed home with the Littles each time—but I vividly remember being impressed the first time I rode with both Hannah and Hunter and witnessed them confidently merge onto a busy interstate and drive in reverse as if they had been doing both for years. I realized that Ryan might be onto something—and it's no surprise that these methods too could be traced back to his CIA operational training.

We even started implementing some of these driving techniques with Ari. At only three years old, he was confident behind the wheel of his Hot Wheels dune buggy because we worked with him on how to shift gears, drive in reverse, and judge depth perception driving up to five miles an hour. We didn't just sit him in the car and say, "Have at it!" We spent time teaching him the different skills so that he is more careful behind the wheel, especially considering his younger sister has been his passenger since she was only fifteen months old. (I know what you're thinking—how could Ryan have possibly convinced me to let our three-year-old drive around our fifteen-month-old? To be honest, I didn't think much of it, as long as she had her helmet on. I suppose that speaks to how far I've come!)

In addition to having confidence while driving a vehicle, it's also critical that your kids have a level of comfort with basic directions and navigation. It's common for teenagers and even adults to rely on GPS technology these days when traveling somewhere, but they lose sight of what's happening around them when they blindly follow the Google Maps voice on their phone or their car navigation system.

One of my favorite episodes of the American version of the TV show *The Office* is the one in which Michael Scott and Dwight Schrute are driving with the assistance of a GPS. Michael trusts the GPS so much that even though a right turn doesn't make sense, he continues until he drives into a lake. Despite seeing the lake, his ability to truly see it and use common sense is thrown out the window. Now, this of course is a humorous, extreme example, but it can happen on a much smaller scale, as I've seen with our oldest daughter.

"I can't remember the address to Nana's house," Hannah said as she and Lena were getting ready to leave the house. "Can you text it to me?" she asked.

"Why do you need the address? You've been there hundreds of times," I said.

"I want to have it, just in case," she told me.

"You've plugged the address into Google Maps every time you've driven there yourself, haven't you?" I asked her.

"Maaaaybe," she replied sheepishly.

"That's why you don't know how to get there. Write down these directions . . ." I said as I started listing off the interstates and exit numbers for her roughly sixty-minute drive to my in-laws.

"Can't you just give me the address?" she pleaded.

"Just follow the signs, and you'll be fine."

I explained to her that until you've driven somewhere and navigated there yourself, through studying a map beforehand and/or familiarizing yourself with landmarks, you'll never learn how to get there on your own. I tried not to be too frustrated with her because although we weren't related by blood, I often saw a lot of myself in her.

I couldn't help but think back to a time when I called my parents for the same kind of guidance. . . .

"I can't find it!" I said alarmingly to my mom and stepdad on the phone while driving to CIA Headquarters for my first day at work. It was nearly 7:00 a.m. at this point, and I was growing more flustered by the minute. My parents had printed out directions to Headquarters from MapQuest—yes this was pre-Garmin and pre–Google Maps—and I found myself pulled over somewhere in the woods of Langley, Virginia, consulting the step-by-step directions in the pre-dawn light that December morning.

What I didn't know was that they hadn't put in the address for the actual CIA Headquarters building and had instead put in a random point on the map nearby. Apparently, they had expected me to read the signs to direct myself there. They had failed to tell me this. My interviews and security processing up to that point had been at satellite buildings, and this was my first time driving into Headquarters. Given that most of my knowledge about the CIA at this point was from the movies, I had mistakenly assumed it was hidden somewhere off the beaten path.

It wasn't.

It was about as obvious as it could be on Route 123 in Langley, with a giant sign out front.

The George Bush Center for Intelligence.

It wasn't the most confidence-building way to start my first day at my new job as a CIA analyst. So like I said, the apple doesn't fall too far.

It wasn't until I began traveling frequently for the CIA that I became more comfortable with the use of maps. We often didn't use technology and stayed off the grid, so it was necessary that I study maps to find my way around new cities and countries. This became a skill I used even on personal travel. I remember traveling with my mom to Paris several years into my CIA career and studying the map each morning to ensure I had areas memorized prior to leaving the hotel. I knew that pulling out a map in public would bring my guard down and signal that I was a tourist, making me an easier target for criminals and thieves.

Reading maps and paying attention to their environment are skills kids can start learning as passengers, which will give them an upper hand later when they start driving. They can observe their surroundings while riding in the car and take in landmarks around them to help them learn routes. One way I do this with Ari is through pointing things out in the car and also telling him what direction we're turning as we're making the turn. Of course, he's a typical kid who enjoys watching movies in the car, but I have a rule that he's only allowed to watch something on our way home from an outing. That way, it guarantees that I've practiced observation and navigation skills with him at least 50 percent of the day's drive, and I can feel less guilty about the amount of screen time I've given him. Naturally, not every day is perfect, and there are times when I cave and give him #allthescreentime, because sometimes it's just about surviving a day with multiple toddlers.

I can't tell you how rewarding it is to hear Ari point out things like, "That's the way to the movie theater," or ask, "Are we going to the park?" which gives me confirmation that the time I've spent talking him through directions ("We're taking a right turn now to go to the park") and pointing out landmarks ("Okay, Ari, get ready to see the farm with the cows on the left") is helping to give him an awareness and orient him to his surroundings in a way that will only improve as he grows older. Indeed, gaining these skills at a young age helps kids focus on taking in the world around them, preparing them to be more security aware.

Key Principles to Teach Your Kids About Practical Security

In addition to teaching surveillance-detection techniques and helping them become confident and comfortable on the road, there are several other practical security awareness principles that you can start implementing with your kids at any age:

1. Don't be predictable. Emphasize to your kids the importance of varying their routine and routes. They shouldn't leave at the same time every day if they can help it, and they shouldn't take the same route to school or work. (Of course, if they ride the bus, there isn't much they can do here.) If someone is watching them, you want to make it more difficult for someone to know where they'll be and when.

2. Lock your doors. When your kids get in their cars, they should immediately lock the doors. Ryan learned this lesson the hard way during a training exercise at the Farm. In just three seconds, an instructor opened his passenger door, reached over to put the car in park, and pulled the keys out of the ignition all while Ryan was stopped at a stop sign. Teach your kids that this can happen quickly. Locking their doors when they get in their vehicle should be second nature to them, just as putting on their seat belts should be. It's also important that your kids realize that this can happen anywhere— not just in places considered dangerous. For example, I was recently watching the nightly news when I heard of an attempted carjacking on I-5 near the Seattle-Tacoma airport. A daughter was driving her father, who was a police officer, to the airport when they heard a multicar crash behind them. Then they saw a man running toward them with a gun in his hand. He grabbed their car door with one hand and pressed his gun up to the window with the other. Thankfully, their doors were locked. The daughter swerved onto the shoulder and drove away as fast as she could. This is a great example of a young woman who not only did the right thing by driving with her doors locked, she also did what she needed to do to get off the X. Her confidence behind the wheel allowed her to see the man coming, and instead of freezing, she quickly sped away just like you would want your child to do in this scenario.

3. Practice memorizing physical descriptions of people, makes and models of vehicles, and license plate numbers. Teach your kids to memorize physical characteristics of people and include what CIA surveillance training refers to as the GRAB: gender, race, age, build. One activity you can do with your kids to help them learn this skill is to people-watch. Take them to a park or a mall and sit on a bench with a view of people passing by. Coach them on the GRAB through pointing out people of various shapes and sizes. Your goal should be for your children to be able to give ballpark estimates of a person's weight and height. If they're mugged or assaulted on the street, would they be able to tell you if the suspect was 185 pounds or 250? Was he 5'7" or 6'3"? If the suspect speeds off in a vehicle, will your kids be able to identify the make and model of that vehicle? And could they do it only by the shape of the vehicle's headlights in the dark? If they think a car is following them, can they read the license plate backward in their rearview mirror while speaking to a 911 operator? This is where those surveillance-detection skills can come in handy.

4. Pay attention to where you sit at restaurants and other venues. When choosing a seat at a table, it's always best to have your back to the wall so that you have the broadest view of the restaurant or café. This allows you to people-watch and to be aware of any situation that could call for getting off the X as quickly as possible. We often turn this into a game with our kids, sometimes even jockeying for the best seat at the table.

5. Put your phone away. Just like you'd never see a spy walking around with his head down looking at his phone, teach your children to put their phones away and observe their surroundings while walking or driving. When Hannah first started driving places alone in the dark, she called Ryan one night as she was walking back to her car because she felt safer on the phone with him. I told him to have her hang up the phone and call him back once she was safely inside her car. We then had a family discussion when she returned home about how being on your phone, whether it's talking to someone or looking at a map, while walking in public can distract you and make you an easy target for a criminal or thief.

6. Pay attention to opportunities for natural look-backs and hone your peripheral vision. An excellent skill to teach your kids is how to discreetly check their surroundings because it gives them the ability to detect someone following them without looking and to ensure their safety. In order to do this, you can actually walk your kids through various places on foot and point out landmarks and areas that offer these opportunities for natural look-backs. A staircase that twists in just the right direction so you can naturally see behind you, and reflections in store windows as you walk by are the types of things you'd point out to them. Even when crossing the street, you can naturally look behind you by looking to your left and right ostensibly for traffic.

While we want our kids to know when someone is following them, sometimes even without looking, there's a key difference between surveillance detection in espionage and in real life. Unlike in intelligence operations, in which you don't want your surveillants to know you've seen them, in real-life scenarios that your kids may encounter, they should 100 percent turn around and look someone in the eye if they think they're being followed. This will throw the person off and help your kids get a better physical description of them. Lastly, if they're in a public place where there are other people around, they can, and should, loudly say, "*Stop following me!*" And if at any time they feel threatened, they should get off the X.

7. You don't have to get out of the car. Something we emphasize to our teenage drivers regularly is that getting out of the car is not a given, even if they're in an accident. This is where their critical-thinking skills and common sense come into play; they'll need to assess each situation. For example, the natural reaction when any driver is rear-ended is to get out, assess the damage, and exchange insurance information with the other driver. That's what we're all taught, right? But what if they're driving alone on an isolated road late at night? In that case, getting out of the car may not be the best choice. There may be security reasons why you shouldn't get out of the car to assess the damage, and you may want to wait for the police.

8. Establish a sound or call that your kids recognize as you in case you're ever separated. When Ryan was down at the Farm, a classmate of his had an ability to make a unique birdlike whistle sound with his mouth. When the instructors asked a question and there was no response, this classmate would make his cricket sound, and laughter would always ensue. After six weeks of practicing every day, Ryan was finally able to imitate this whistle but in a wider, much lower range. At the time, he thought he would use the whistle in the same way his colleague did—it was a great way to lighten the mood and get laughs. He later realized on a boardwalk in Europe with the three Bigs, who were five, three, and one at the time, that the whistle was a great tool for keeping track of them and giving instruction. The kids rode their wooden balance bikes ahead of him, and they quickly learned that one trill meant stop and two trills meant come back. Having a unique sound like this just for your family sensitizes your kids' ears to what's around them. For example, several years ago when the Bigs were in elementary school, Ryan would often wait outside their classrooms when he went to pick them up, and he'd do his whistle. No one else in the room would even notice the sound, but the kids always heard it and knew Daddy was there waiting for them. If you, like me, can't do a unique whistle with your mouth, there are all sorts of small duck calls or actual whistles you can buy and test out. Find what works for your family. As for us, the whistle continued to be useful for Ryan wherever he went with the Bigs, and he still uses it to this day with the Bigs and the Littles when we're out and about. And it even works for the dogs.

It's not until your kids start learning these security-awareness techniques that they'll really know what to look for and begin to see the world in a different way. Indeed, they'll begin to see things they've been missing on a daily basis. Has that car always been parked there? Is that the same man I saw this morning at the Starbucks across town? The more they train their eyes to look for these things, the more natural this skill set will become for them. Likewise, the younger you teach your children these tools, the better security awareness they'll have throughout the rest of their lives.

CHAPTER SEVEN

DEFEND YOURSELF

What to Do When Danger Finds You

We've discussed how to teach your kids to get off the X and be more security aware, but now it's time to discuss the possibility that despite your kids' best efforts, they might find themselves in a situation in which they have no choice but to defend themselves.

If your children find themselves in a fight-for-their-life situation, it's important that you've had discussions with them about the fragility of the human body. Your children need to understand that what they see in the movies and in video games is not realistic, and in fact, it's the opposite. Real life isn't like the movies, in which someone can be punched ten, twenty, or even thirty times and get back up. This just doesn't happen. Ryan regularly reminds the Bigs of this when we're watching a movie at home. He'll actually pause the movie so that we can discuss it, and he'll remind the kids that this is not real life. In fact, there are instances in the news where a person is killed by much lesser trauma, sometimes only one punch. A person can't take being punched in the face over and over again.

Nor can they successfully fight two, three, four, or five people at a time or be shot and still save the world. These scenes aren't realistic. One punch, one kick to the head, or someone coming at you with a knife is all it can take to end your life.

It also helps if kids understand that there's a reason for weight classes in wrestling and martial arts. Over the years, I've watched Ryan explain this to the Bigs numerous times. What inevitably follows is a conversation, usually led by our teenage son, about who would win in fights with various people we know.

"So who would win in a fight? You or Uncle Bobby?" or "Do you think I could take so-and-so?" It's not just conversations, though; sometimes this also leads to an actual wrestling match in our living room (which, funnily enough, is taking place right now as I sit writing this at our kitchen table). These wrestling matches and sparring have taken place for as long as I've known Ryan and the Bigs. I've watched him sneak up on the kids in the kitchen and try to put them in a headlock or some other hold. They'll wrestle and spar all while he's teaching them the importance of quick reflexes and skills on how to fight back. When I first saw him doing this with the Bigs, I remember thinking it was playful. I had no idea how much thought and technique was behind it. Now we implement those same tactics with the Littles through playful wrestling, often trapping them between our legs and having them use their own strength to wiggle out. When they whine and say they can't do it, we tell them that they're strong and they can. This helps teach them the motor skills to learn how to break free of different types of holds while at the same time building their confidence when they actually do get out. As they grow older and gain a better understanding of these concepts, we don't let them win as easily so that they can start to grasp the concept of weight classes. We stress to them that motor skills and technique can only take them so far, which is why a fight scenario is one that should be avoided unless absolutely necessary.

These types of conversations and hands-on experience help us hammer the point home that even though someone is a star fighter, if they're outweighed, the fighter likely doesn't stand a chance. A 200-pound fighter against a 150-pound fighter is no fight. You can take the best MMA fighter in the world, and if you put him up against two other men who outweigh him by thirty or forty pounds each, he'll most likely lose, despite his training and skills. For example, in 2016, the Olympic judo fighter Dirk Van Tichelt was mugged and assaulted by two criminals on the street in Rio de Janeiro just after winning the bronze medal. Van Tichelt was a professional martial arts athlete who trained his entire life, yet somehow he found himself the victim of a mugging, demonstrating that even the most experienced fighters can lose under the right circumstances.

I remember finding these real-life conversations with the Bigs, who weren't so big at the time, unsettling early on in my relationship with Ryan.

"Are you sure we should be talking to them about this stuff?" I'd ask. "There's so much bad stuff in the world; we should protect them from it for as long as we can and just let them enjoy life," I'd tell him. Over the years, however, I've realized that not just knowledge, but preparation, is power. And just like Ryan has a way of discussing survival techniques and end-of-the-world scenarios with the kids in a non-alerting way, there's also an appropriate way to discuss with our kids things like the fragility of the human body and how to defend ourselves without taking away the joy of childhood. It's possible for these concepts to coexist.

Ideally, your kids won't find themselves in one of these

fight-for-their-life scenarios. Instead, it's my hope that they'll develop enough intelligence and instincts to identify the X and steer clear of it, but in the event that they can't, I want to help you prepare them.

Debunking Assumptions About Spies and Weapons

When most people hear that I'm a former CIA spy, they assume I've had elaborate fighting and weapons training and that I carried weapons on me at all times. It's true that there are some situations in which CIA officers carry weapons, but more often than not, they don't. There are a variety of reasons for this, like the fact that they're working undercover as diplomats and businesspeople, for example. And like I mentioned, if a CIA officer has to pull out a weapon, then he's done something wrong. Because I was an analyst, I had next to no experience with weapons during my time at the CIA, despite having spent the latter half of my career doing clandestine operations. And when it comes to our kids having knives or really knowing much about weapons in general, I tend to shy away from it because, quite frankly, it's something I've had very little exposure to in general.

Ryan, on the other hand, underwent extensive weapons training at the CIA on a variety of weapons, including Glocks, M4s, and the entire Kalashnikov family of weapons—everything from the Dragunov sniper rifle to the everyday AK-47. He learned how to shoot, dismantle, and clean them all, inside and out. While it's unlikely a CIA officer will need to use a weapon, the Agency trains its officers for worst-case scenarios in all aspects of its curriculum. They also train with repetition. You'll hear me give a lot of examples about how the CIA isn't like its portrayal in films, but here's a case in which it's exactly right: When you see people struggling to put their keys into the door or the ignition, that's realistic. In an emergency or high-stress situation, people lose their ability to conduct fine motor skills. That's why the CIA focuses on training with repetitive gross motor skills, meaning big movements, for all the weapons in which it trains its officers. That's also why the karambit knife (often referred to as a "claw") is useful, because it can be used in an up-and-down defensive gross-motor-skill action. In his training, Ryan also learned of the need for an equalizer to level the playing field. It can be a knife, pepper spray, and in some cases, a more substantial weapon.

It's not all about weapons, though—after all, we're not in the business of training kids to be MMA fighters or CIA assassins. It's about teaching your kids to defend themselves using whatever means are available to them, be it a tool or a makeshift weapon, specifically if they're in a situation in which they have no option but to fight to survive. One of the best ways to teach this is through a gradual-learning approach that introduces the use of tools before advancing to an understanding of how tools can be used as weapons—an approach that I admittedly haven't always been on board with and at times still disagree on with Ryan.

Finding Our Family's Balance When It Comes to Self-Defense

"Don't forget your neck knives!" Ryan yelled to the Bigs as they were running out the front door. Sometimes they grabbed them and ran out the door with no pushback, and other times, they reminded us that they're typical teenagers when they rolled their eyes and said, "Daaaad, do we have to? We'll be fine." They were heading out for a hike, and Ryan preferred that they have a knife with them to use as a tool and for protection.

"Yes, you have to. Either wear the neck knife or you're not going," he said firmly, and the complaints stopped there.

It wasn't always like this with the Bigs. Of course, they were much younger when I first met them, so they weren't carrying knives around their necks while hiking, mountain-biking, or doing anything else, for that matter. They were, however, using knives as tools.

Is whittling with a pocketknife appropriate for an eight-year-old? I asked myself when I first saw Hunter doing it. With zero parenting experience under my belt, I wasn't so sure, and it certainly made me nervous. I'd grown up with a dad who was a safety manager, and I still remember when he made my sister and me watch a video about how cigarette lighters could blow up in your pocket after finding one in hers. As you can imagine, knives—of any sort—weren't something we were introduced to as kids in my family. Ryan, on the other hand, was an Eagle Scout and had carried a Swiss Army knife in his pocket from elementary school through high school, so it's not surprising how calm and measured he was when it came to knives and other tools. After all, this, just like everything else about his parenting style, was carefully considered, deliberate, and, from his perspective, very safe.

To say this mind-set and level of comfort has taken some getting used to for me would be an understatement. I vividly remember early in our dating relationship when I added "pocketknives" to the mental list of things I observed Ryan do with the Bigs that I planned to do differently with my future children, right there along with motorcycles. If Ryan and I married, he'd have to make some adjustments. The train may have already left the station with the Bigs, but there was plenty of time to get on the same page before we had kids together, I told myself.

Fast-forward nearly eight years to when Ryan came home from a business trip to Europe.

"I have a surprise for you!" he said excitedly to Ari, who of course put out his hands and closed his eyes right on cue.

"What is it?" he said in an excited whisper.

"It's your very first knife," Ryan said. "It's called an Opinel . . . it's French."

My eyes immediately darted to him. It was just as much a surprise to me as it was to Ari.

"You can't use it yet, but you can hold the box and look inside the plastic cover," Ryan continued. "When you're a little older, I'll show you how to use it."

"A lot older," I added.

Later that night after we put the Littles to bed, when my emotions weren't running quite as high, I decided to broach the topic with Ryan.

"You know, I really feel like we should have had a discussion about giving Ari his first knife," I began.

"Well, I saw it in Vienna, and I've never seen one with a black blade like this one. I knew I'd get him one eventually, so I went ahead and picked it up," he said.

"Yes, but then you gave it to him . . . without even telling me you had bought it first," I said, remaining calm. And then I said it: "You went rogue." This is a phrase Ryan and I often use when one of us decides to go "off script" or do something unilaterally, like have a serious conversation with any of the kids without coordinating it with the other first. We have an agreement to discuss any serious decisions or conversations beforehand to ensure we're both on the same page.

Because we have different strengths and parenting styles in our own right, we find that a coordinated approach, even if one parent ends up doing most of the talking, will be more balanced and impactful than if one of us forges ahead on our own, or goes rogue, so to speak. Of course, sometimes coordinating isn't possible. For example, you may find yourself on a car ride with one of the kids when a serious topic naturally comes up. In those moments we have to think on our feet and then discuss the topic afterward with the other person. If one of us didn't use the best language or cover all the points we'd like, then we come up with a plan for how we'll revisit the issue either together or separately. When we invoke the "You went rogue" claim, it's almost like a safe word, and the responsible party understands and *almost* always offers up an apology without question. (I say *almost* because life is messy, and let's be honest, there are times when neither of us wants to apologize.)

"You're right; I did. I'm sorry," he said.

"Thanks. . . . I'm just not ready to introduce him to knives," I replied.

"Well, but we're not giving it to him yet," he protested.

"Yes, but now you've created this magical curiosity surrounding it, and I don't like that. I just wish we could have talked about it beforehand. You know I don't like knives."

"I know. I wasn't thinking. I'm sorry," he said again. "But the more we demystify it, the less curious about it he'll be, and he'll actually be safer." He couldn't help but defend his case.

"I know that's what you think, but he's three years old. We're just not there yet, so let's cool it, please." And that was that . . . for now, at least.

-RYAN-

HOW AND WHY I INTRODUCED POCKETKNIVES AND OTHER TOOLS TO THE BIGS

Here's the stark reality that I, along with all other parents, faced when I first became a father: I'm not able to be with the kids at all times to protect them and keep them safe. Because of this reality, I want to know that I've done enough to prepare them and teach them so that they have the best chance to get off the X, defend themselves, and make it back home. As part of this endeavor, I began teaching the Bigs how to properly use pocketknives when they each turned five years old. I first introduced them to basic pocketknives for kids—"my first Opinel knife" and "my first Victorinox Swiss Army knife," neither of which has a sharp point, just rounded tips like a butter knife. I taught them how to whittle wood with these knives. Whittling is something most kids love or learn to love if given the opportunity within a safe environment, and if they understand the rules of using a pocketknife.

At first, I started with long thin sticks for roasting marshmallows and hot dogs over the campfire. There's a certain joy that comes from carving your first of many marshmallow and hot dog sticks.

"You made this stick," I would tell the kids. "You carved the point and made something from your own hands. You accomplished something—doesn't that feel good?" I'd ask them as they pushed the marshmallow or hot dog onto the stick to roast it over the fire. This has become a rite of passage.

In the time that followed, I taught the Bigs to carve larger spears and walking sticks. They even carved small utensils and tools out of wood. They also learned how to properly open boxes and packages, cut rope, and do other things that need a knife or something sharp to complete the task. Additionally, I'd like to point out—these early pocketknives were always kept somewhere safe and out of reach. They were brought out only under adult supervision, and the rules were always reinforced. Occasionally (and inevitably) accidents happened and the kids would make minor cuts on their hands. Even Dad, who is extremely experienced, sometimes cut himself by accident, and this is where proper Band-Aid and first aid procedures came in (as was discussed in chapter 4). This is also why it's so important that your kids understand the uses and power of knives and cutting and have some basic familiarity, so that they keep themselves safe (for example, if they're at a friend's house, and the friend doesn't know what they're doing and starts to play with a knife). You want your kids to know the rules and the proper uses, and to be safe. If they've never held a pocketknife or been taught the rules or what to do, this leaves them unprepared, vulnerable, and potentially in a dangerous situation if they find themselves alone or without their parents' supervision.

As the Bigs grew older, I introduced them to more complicated and sophisticated knives, as well as the concept that in addition to using a knife as a tool, they could also use it for protection, like the neck knife Christina mentioned (the karambit). Because the knife's blade is curved (the most efficient form in nature, similar to a tiger's claw), if someone tried to take it from you, the tip of the blade could still reach the attacker's hand and inflict even more damage while they're trying to wrestle the knife away. The benefit of carrying a neck knife is that it gives someone extra confidence and peace of mind, and it really is a deterrent. To put it frankly, the karambit looks scary and badass. If you ever had to whip it out (hopefully that's something that would never happen), just the sight of it in your hand would likely make someone walk away. You don't mess with a karambit. In addition, because it's a neck knife, no one knows it's there. Someone could take your purse or your bag, or make you empty your pockets, or throw you in the back of a van, but your neck knife is still hidden on your person and ready for when you need it.

Another tool I taught the kids from an early age was how to use the longbow for archery. I began training Hannah and Hunter in Switzerland when they were three and five years old. They started out with simple, small beginner's bows and arrows and a large target. Over the years, they've worked on perfecting their skills. Using instinct (rather than aim) to shoot their arrows exactly where they wanted them, whether they or their targets were stationary or moving. They regularly played archery games at their grandparents' house, where they took advantage of their several acres of land. Hannah became increasingly enthralled with archery, especially after reading and watching the Hunger Games series; she wanted to be like Katniss and was an extremely accurate shot. Lena wanted to be like Merida from Disney's *Brave*, and Hunter, well, he was a natural right off the bat. The girls still love archery but have drifted away from it as teenagers. Hunter, on the other hand, eventually wanted to move up from a longbow to a compound bow. For his fifteenth birthday, I bought him a Mathews compound bow. We now regularly shoot our compound bows together, and in addition to improving his archery skills, which can be used in a survival context or in self-defense, it's a great way to spend quality time with each other.

At the end of the day, it's about ensuring I've done everything I can to teach the kids to defend themselves, if necessary. This includes introducing tools at fairly young ages that can also be used as weapons later, if the situation calls for it. When done appropriately and safely, this can be a great way to prepare your kids for dangerous situations when you can't be there to protect them.

You have to admit, he's pretty convincing, right? While initially the thought of a kid carving something out of wood with his own pocketknife seemed wildly inappropriate and even borderline dangerous to me (and perhaps to you too?), once I understood Ryan's gradual approach and the thought process behind it, it started to make sense. Now, I'm not saying your kids have to carry knives or any weapon. Ever. Please hear me again: Your kids do not need to carry knives or *any* weapon, nor should they have access to any weapons in your home. If you/or your partner have any sort of weapons, please ensure they are locked up properly in a safe to which only you know the combination.

While Ryan's approach may make more sense to me now, I wouldn't say that I'm 100 percent on board. I tend to think that he sometimes introduces these ideas a bit too young—like when he told our three-year-old that he bought him his very own pocketknife for when he's a little older—but between the two of us, I think we strike the right balance. And really, I'm thankful for the more traditional spy background he brings to the table when it comes to this topic, because it balances out my data-driven, analytic approach to parenting.

Key Principles to Teach Your Kids About Self-Defense

At the end of the day, I believe in preparing and training our kids for the unexpected. I want them to know how to fight off an attacker if they find themselves in such a situation—although I hope and pray they never do. Ryan's measured approach of introducing them to tools and the fragility of the human body allows for your kids to build knowledge, skills, and comfort with these concepts over time. Here are some principles to focus on as you teach your kids about self-defense:

1. **Look for an equalizer.** If knives make you, like me, uncomfortable, then take them off the table. If your kids are in a fight situation, help them to understand that they can use anything around them as a weapon to defend themselves. For example, I'm sitting at my desk right now as I write. If an attacker were to come into my room at this moment, the first thing I would look to use against them is my desk lamp. Teach your kids to find objects that can be used as "improvised defensive tools," because when they can't get off the X and their back is against the wall, they'll need to reach for what's at arm's length.

They'll need an equalizer; whether it's something they carry on their person or something around them that they find within seconds that they can use as a makeshift weapon to thwart an attacker, they need something to (a) act as a deterrent, (b) put some distance between them and the attacker, or (c) wound or immobilize the attacker. It doesn't need to be something that is characterized as a weapon; it could be a stapler or a hammer, or even a pen. It's not necessarily the item itself but more how it's used, and it can be more deadly than any pocketknife. That equalizer could also be their own fists or knees—I highly recommend they participate in a self-defense class so that they can learn other basic ways to defend themselves with their own body. It's important, however, that your kids understand that even after learning these defensive techniques, if they're against someone who outweighs them or they're outnumbered, they're at a severe disadvantage. For this reason they should use everything available to them, and if there are no objects to grab as makeshift weapons, they should use their voice to scream as loud as possible for help.

2. Seize opportunities to spar and wrestle with your kids. We've discussed the importance of teaching your kids to have quick reflexes, and a great way to practice this while they're young is to spar and wrestle with them. This, of course, can become more advanced and intense as they get older, but don't be afraid to start young. When done in a playful way, it can be fun for kids, and they don't even realize that you're teaching them how to defend themselves in the real world. If this isn't your thing for whatever reason, then you can consider enrolling your child in a martial arts class or encouraging them to join the wrestling team at school, for example.

3. Emphasize the fragility of the human body through examples in film and real life. As we discussed, it's critical for kids to understand how little it actually takes to injure or even kill the human body. They're surrounded by so many unrealistic examples in movies and video games that it can be difficult for them to grasp just how fragile we are. Help them understand so they know that what they see in the movies isn't real life. At the same time, we want this knowledge to empower them, not frighten them, so it's important that you do this in a way that educates them and that you tie it in with what you learned in chapter 5 about getting off the X. You can pause movies like Ryan does to discuss this concept with your kids, or if it's age appropriate for your children, you can share actual news stories with them.

Your kids need these skills and defensive knowledge not just to fend off an attacker or even to prepare for the zombie apocalypse but also because, as I'll discuss in the following chapters, it makes them well rounded, a trait that can help them in a variety of ways in life. Moreover, this training and focus will help them become confident and give them a realistic understanding of self-defense techniques. They'll be security aware and have an edge over their peers, which in turn will bring you more comfort, peace, and confidence that the kids will be prepared as much as possible for any situation that they'll encounter.

CHAPTER EIGHT

YOU ME, SAME SAME

How to Find Common Ground with Others

"Okay, let's practice again," I heard Ryan say to Hannah at the kitchen table. I was sitting in the other room, carefully observing how he prepared his anxious sixth grader for being the new kid at school once again. It was something I thought the kids would have been used to by then—moving and starting at a new school. After all, Ryan had already done multiple overseas tours in different locations prior to his divorce, but it never got any easier for them, especially for Hannah, his reserved, kindhearted, oldest child. Each time, Ryan role-played with her, helping to remind her of the best ways to connect with others and make new friends.

"Okay," said Hannah. "I'll start. . . . Hi, I'm Hannah. What's your name?"

"Hi, I'm Katie," Ryan said.

"Can I sit with you for lunch?" Hannah asked timidly.

"Sure."

"Did you have a fun summer?" Hannah asked.

"Stop," said Ryan, breaking character. "You don't ever want to start with a yes-no question. Then the person can say yes or no, and that's where the conversation ends. You want to ask an opened-ended question that makes her share what she did over the summer. Then, depending on what you learn about her, you can use that information to build rapport. Let's try again."

"Hi, Hannah, sure, you can sit with me," Ryan said, restarting the role-play as Katie, the sixth-grade girl.

"Thanks . . . so . . . what sorts of things did you do over the summer?" Hannah asked.

"Perfect!" Ryan said, breaking character again. "That's exactly what I meant." And then back into character: "I did a lot of swimming."

"That sounds fun. I love to swim too. Where did you swim?"

"My family has a boat that we take out on the lake," Katie said.

"That's so cool! My grandparents have one that I've been going on since I was little. I love to go tubing with my siblings and cousins," Hannah said. This was an example of another technique Ryan had taught her, called "give to get." Once someone gives you a little and you start to connect, it's okay to give a little about you to help further the conversation along and build rapport.

"Tubing is the best!" Ryan said again as Katie. Then, breaking character, "This was great, Hannah, and it's exactly what you should do tomorrow. What's another question you could ask after you mention your family?"

"Ummm . . . I could ask about her family?" Hannah asked.

"Exactly. Maybe something like, 'Do you have a big or small family?'" Ryan coached her. "Remember not to ask yes-no questions and to build on whatever you learn about them. Be sure to remember names too. That way, when you see them again later in the day or the following day, you can greet them with their name. That makes people feel special and helps solidify your new bond with them."

I sat with a look of both amazement and confusion on the couch. Ryan saw the look, and when Hannah got up to go to her room, he came over to me.

"What's that face?" he asked.

"Are you teaching them 'You Me, Same Same'?" I asked him point-blank. I was pretty sure I recognized the technique, but I had never seen it done outside a CIA training or operational setting.

He smiled.

"Yes," he said. "It's the perfect way to teach them how to connect with others. At the end of the day, life is all about relationships, and they need to know how to build them."

The Power of Building Relationships

It wasn't the first time I had heard Ryan say life is all about relationships, and it certainly wouldn't be the last, but it was fair to say I had never considered using this technique meant for espionage in my kids' daily lives. In fact, before I met Ryan, I chalked up the technique as nothing more than a somewhat slimy way of schmoozing and means to an end, albeit a patriotic one.

When most people think of the CIA, they think about what we've discussed up to this point—security, safety, and trusting your gut. They may think of James Bond as suave, but they probably haven't considered the vast amount of training in social skills that goes into creating such a smoothly operating CIA officer. This type of training and experience has helped shape our parenting style in the same way that the more physical field tradecraft has.

Just before meeting Ryan, I took part in operational training to prepare for my field assignment in the DO. The first class was an eight-week introductory course that DO officers went through immediately after starting at the Agency. Our cadre of eight analysts joined the green DO officers as they learned about the organization writ large for the first time, and together, we all learned things like how to bump a target, debrief an asset, and write an operational cable, which was essentially a summary of your asset meeting that you sent back to Headquarters.

After reading cables and writing papers on a regular basis as an analyst for several years by this point, I sailed through the cable-writing and debriefing portions of the training. Strangely enough, I found the training on how to bump a target (making a moment seem natural, like a chance encounter, or a "bump") remarkably similar to rushing a sorority in college, although I'm sure if I shared that with my instructors they would have insisted this was *much* more complex. Role-playing was common in DO training, and we took part in fictitious diplomatic receptions for training purposes. Before entering the room, we were given a photo of our target and a few details about him or her—things like hobbies, interests, likes, and dislikes. Our goal at the reception was to use the information on the card to identify the target, strike up a meaningful conversation, and ultimately secure a second meeting.

Similarly, in my sorority house, we received a photo and biographic details of the girls who were rushing prior to their arrival. We then lined up according to how the girls would arrive. If all went as planned, you were paired up with the girl about whom you had read before the arrivals. Sometimes it didn't work because the girls were out of order, but when it did, it was gold. You created an immediate connection with her when you casually brought up what you had learned on the card.

"My sorority sister [fill in the blank] loved meeting you yesterday. She mentioned you did theater in high school. I did too!" I said to one such girl.

"Oh wow, really? That's so cool. Which shows were you in?"

And so the conversation continued. Girls loved feeling like someone had told you great things about them, but in reality, no one told you anything. Or if you were really smooth, you would casually steer the conversation in the direction of one of their interests and feign surprise when they said they loved kickboxing too. In reality, you weren't surprised by anything. The note card had information the girls had shared about themselves when they decided to rush a sorority as well as tidbits your sorority sisters learned about them in previous meetings. In short, it told you everything you needed to know before you ever saw her. It was the perfect setup because with so many girls visiting the chapter, it was impossible to talk to the person who met them at the previous party. In fact, we met so many girls, it was difficult to keep them straight. After a while, the Tiffany bracelets, Burberry scarves, and Uggs started to run together.

At the CIA, we approached targets and developed relationships with them in a similar way. We called it the "You Me, Same Same" approach. Finding common ground created a connection and helped conversation flow. Of course, in these situations you wouldn't say that you'd learned something about them from someone else.

After you bumped a target and made a connection, your goal was to secure a second meeting. You did this by connecting with them over a shared interest. It was also important to get them talking. By and large, people like to talk about themselves. It's common for people to walk away from meeting someone thinking, *"Wow, I really liked that person,"* when in reality, they did most of the talking themselves. Connecting with someone on a subject they love and peppering them with questions about themselves—so long as it's done naturally—can leave a person feeling positive about the conversation. From there, you met with the target regularly and developed a relationship. You became "friends" with the person—took them out to restaurants, concerts, golfing, you name it. I knew some operations officers who took their assets skydiving or race car driving! Sometimes this development and building rapport lasted up to several months, but it could also last years. Not only were you building trust during this time, you were also assessing the target, learning their motivations, vulnerabilities, weaknesses, vices, political ideology, and so on. Once you progressed in the relationship, you took all the assessment information and rapport that you'd built with the person and used it for the eventual "pitch," which essentially meant officially asking them to have a clandestine relationship with the CIA—that is, spy on behalf of the United States. If an operations officer did their job correctly and created enough rapport and a solid relationship, then the answer should have always been yes. Instructors compared it to a marriage proposal. You wouldn't propose to someone unless you were 99.9 percent sure they would say yes. In the same way, you wouldn't pitch a person unless you were 99.9 percent sure they would agree to it.

To be perfectly honest, these exercises made me feel smarmy—first at nineteen years old in my sorority and then years later sitting in my CIA training class. So this was how all these DO guys had been winning me over when they asked me out on dates! While I had fallen for their tradecraft on several occasions, more often than not, I encountered operations officers who didn't seem genuine in their attempts to use the You Me, Same Same approach in their operations. During a Headquarters rotation to the DO, I sat in weekly operational meetings and heard about plans to approach targets, and sometimes they just didn't sit well with me. Bumping a target in a doctor's office waiting room and using the fact that both of your parents have multiple sclerosis as common ground? Hmm. That felt a little gross. Pretending to be a nuclear target's friend for days at a conference, connecting with her as female scientists, only to tell her it was all a ruse so that you could ask her to commit espionage on your behalf by the end of the week? Yikes. These types of attempts at You Me, Same Same didn't just make me feel smarmy and question the tradecraft, they often failed, just like these two real examples did. When operations officers used this technique in a manipulative way or pretended to be someone they weren't, the relationship wasn't able to take off in the same way it would have if the officer sought to find *genuine* common ground. It wasn't until I met Ryan that I realized it could be done differently, and as a result, more successfully.

For example, on a foreign assignment where Ryan interacted with people of several nations on a daily basis, he proved his ability to build rapport with just about anyone from any country, in any language. This was because he recognized that at the end of the day, we're more alike than we might think. The news and social media often remind us of our differences, whether political, cultural, or otherwise, but Ryan seeks to find commonality between us. The key to his success, however, isn't only that he recognizes this—it's that he is easily the most well-rounded person I've ever met. When he wasn't able to connect with someone based on an interest he already had, he took interest in one of their interests. And on some occasions, he could be quite creative.

-RYAN-

SCUBA DIVING FOR
THE GREATER GOOD

While serving overseas, we identified a company that was heavily involved in illicit activities with a country of extreme interest. We needed to find a way to access this highly sought-after intelligence, so the Station targeter conducted a deep dive on the company to see which individuals would most likely have access to the information we needed. Once he narrowed it down to three people, we came together to dissect their entire lives—finances, jobs, social media, schooling, and so on. From there, we zeroed in on one person who we thought would be most receptive to an approach. We did an even deeper dive on this one person to learn as much about him as possible, and the Chief of Station chose me as the officer to go after him.

There's a number of ways that I could have targeted this person—or any person in an operation like this—particularly because we had so much information about the individual's life. I knew I wanted to find an interest that we shared so that we could build a real connection. As I scanned through his interests and hobbies several times, I kept landing on scuba diving. True, I had never been diving before, but it was something I had always wanted to try. I wouldn't have to feign interest or excitement. Hell, I could even become legitimately passionate about diving, if given the opportunity. And thus, my ops plan was formed.

I immediately enrolled in scuba diving lessons and joined the local scuba club, where I planned to approach the target. We knew he loved diving to the point that he considered it one of his life's passions. The first night I showed up at the scuba club, the target was there. I had preplanned my entire conversation—knowing so much about him in advance helped me develop a plan and strategy for building rapport. I decided it would be a calculated discussion; the conversation would start with A and make its way to Z, with me leading and guiding the conversation along.

The meeting went just as I had hoped. The conversation hit all the points I had planned, and I gradually built rapport around our mutual interests. My sole purpose was to get the target to like me and be fascinated by me as an individual, making him want to see me again and form a friendship. Over the course of several months, we continued to meet on a weekly basis, sometimes for lunch and other times for dinner. I got to know him as a person and even met his wife and kids. During these first several months, I never once brought up his job. Not once. If he mentioned it, I took the opportunity to ask questions and elicit information from him, but I was careful not to ever be the first person to introduce the topic.

My focus instead was on using the time over the next several months to continue to connect with him as a person and a friend. At the same time, I was naturally learning about his motivations, ideologies, and vulnerabilities—anything that may make him interested in a clandestine relationship with an intelligence service. While that was the end goal, the focus was always on how to leverage those shared interests to build a genuine relationship in order to get us there.

As Ryan demonstrated in his scuba diving efforts, in order to reach the point where you're ready to confidently pitch a person for an official clandestine relationship with the CIA, or what's called a recruitment, you need to be able to build rapport and form a relationship of trust with that person over time. The basis of that relationship should be genuine common ground. However, you can't connect with someone on common interests if your interests are limited, and in real life, you likely won't be in a situation where you have the time and money to take up a new hobby just to connect with someone. That's why it's important to emphasize the idea of well-roundedness for your kids as early as possible—they should know something about everything and everything about something.

One of the best ways to teach your kids this concept is to model it for them. Ryan, for example, speaks four languages, plays multiple instruments, enjoys a variety of sports, cooks and bakes from scratch—the list goes on. No, really, it does. With this impressive portfolio of skills and interests, he can pull from just about anything when meeting someone to find areas on which to connect. It wasn't just common interests on which we connected on our first date, though; I was drawn to him because his array of interests fascinated me. I also spoke multiple languages, but I sure as hell couldn't do most of the other things I learned about him. I couldn't help but laugh when he told me he knew how to play the Irish pennywhistle. Of course he did. And not just any pennywhistle. He played one made by hand out of cocobolo wood by someone named Erik the Flutemaker in Florida. *Who is this guy?* I thought to myself. I immediately knew I wanted to know him more.

My fascination with Ryan continued when I met his kids, and it was clear to me that he had also instilled the concept of being well rounded in them. Let's be honest, I hadn't met any kids under ten who knew how to ride motorcycles, shoot arrows, and ski. As someone whose life had revolved around her career up until that point, I was embarrassed to admit that the Bigs had many more hobbies and skills than I did as a nearly thirty-year-old adult. During those years of dating and early marriage, I became less career-obsessed, no doubt taking cues from Ryan, who had an amazing ability to put family above his career, while at the same time not sacrificing professional success. I found that I had more free time for interests and hobbies once I was away from the hustle and bustle of Headquarters and the Washington, D.C., area. I chose to fill most of it by spending time with Ryan and the kids doing many of the activities they enjoyed. It wasn't until after Ari was born and I became a stay-at-home mom that I started to struggle with my identity. Who was I if I didn't have my career? Who was I if I wasn't traveling to Africa throughout the year? What hobbies did I have apart from Ryan? Apart from the Bigs? Apart from my new baby? Sometimes I felt like the most interesting part about me was my husband.

I shared this feeling with Ryan often, and at first he didn't seem to get it.

"Of course you have hobbies," he said. "You like to hike . . . make leather . . . shoot bow and arrow . . ."

I couldn't help but laugh.

"Those are all *your* hobbies," I said. "I've never made anything out of leather." It seemed he was getting my management of his leather business confused with the actual talent required to hand-sew a wallet or handbag out of leather.

"Well, yeah, but you like those things too . . . and you could learn to make leather," he said, still clearly not getting it.

It was true I liked those things, but they didn't feel like mine. That's not to say people can't share hobbies and interests—after all, that's what the whole concept of You Me, Same Same is about, but what I really needed was to find my passions and interests in this stage of life. What was *my* scuba diving?

The early postpartum days when I was surviving on extremely small amounts of sleep and extremely large amounts of caffeine hardly seemed like the time to take up new hobbies. Nonetheless, I knew I was going to go crazy if I didn't get out of the house. I connected with a stroller-friendly exercise group in a nearby town. I'm not sure if it was the postpartum anxiety that made exercise feel so good or if it was because for the first time since my career I found something I was good at and truly enjoyed. Maybe it was a combination of both. Within months, I was training to become an instructor, and two years later, when Ari was two years old and Gigi was one, I started my own fitness company for prenatal and postpartum mothers in my small mountain town. I discovered that in addition to loving fitness, which may have been the shocker of all since I used every excuse in the book to avoid running in gym class growing up, I loved creating a community for local mothers to connect on shared interests. Here were mothers connecting over nighttime wake-ups, breastfeeding, bottle-feeding, potty training, you name it. It was also a safe place for moms to share joys in their lives as well as struggles. Moms felt like they had finally found a place where other women could relate to the monumental changes their lives—and their bodies—had just experienced. It was the epitome of You Me, Same Same, and it all stemmed from me finding something I enjoyed.

This is one example of an interest I've taken up at this stage of my life, and it happens to be the one in which I've chosen to dive the deepest. However, over the years, I've dabbled in several different areas in an effort to make myself a well-rounded adult and parent, everything from taking a pie-baking class to attending architectural tours to learning how to wakesurf. At times it's felt uncomfortable to start new hobbies in my thirties, and that's why I think it's so important to instill this concept in your kids at an early age. We can help them to acquire a variety of interests early on in life, and we can also teach them the joy in discovering new hobbies at any age by modeling it ourselves. Having a multitude of interests and then learning to use those interests to connect with others can help your kids throughout their lives when it comes to making friends, solving disputes, nailing a job interview, conquering the dating world, and so on.

Where Should You Start?

Begin by exposing your kids to a variety of skills as early as possible. This is the best way to lay the groundwork for teaching them the You Me, Same Same concept. Consider the types of skills that may be useful in life to make them well rounded as well as skills that interest them. You may consider things like archery, motorcycles, sailing, hiking, camping, cooking, athletics, computer programming, music, crafting, and more. These don't have to be skills that you yourself have. You can find a class for your kids to take alone if they're interested, or you can take up a new interest together. Seeing you learn something new with them can demonstrate that it's never too late to learn and add to your repertoire.

As a bonus, many of these skills can be used not only to connect with people but also in other areas we've discussed, like survival. For example, Lena is prepared to hunt her own food using a bow and arrow if the situation calls for it, and like I mentioned, her ability to hit bull's-eye after bull's-eye also wowed her classmates and teachers. This made her fascinating to others and gave her an interesting hobby that she could use to connect with them. Additionally, the kids' experience riding motorcycles gives them talking points they may use when meeting someone. Hannah's motorcycle endorsement also prepares her for a way to get out of Dodge in the event of a natural disaster. In full transparency, though, I still struggle with the idea of putting my babies (because they'll *always* be my babies) on motorcycles. It's an area where Ryan and I often agree to disagree. That said, I see the value in it from multiple angles, but the jury is still out on whether I'll allow the Littles to ride one solo before they're adults. If this is you too, don't get hung up on motorcycles. There are so many other interests and hobbies you can explore with your kids, and they don't need to be limited to physical skills.

Exercising your brain is just as important, which is why, for example, we recommend your kids do daily readings, of your or their choosing. In our home, we prefer the Harvard classics and the *Economist*. Introducing your kids to the classics is an excellent way to provide them with ample opportunity to connect with people across the globe, and exposing them to literature discussing current events is critical to opening their eyes to the rest of the world. The goal with all of these skills is to help your kids excel socially by giving them an abundance of topics to discuss with others.

Once they're well rounded—or on their way to becoming so— you can teach them how to use those interests to communicate effectively with others. Role-play with them in the same way Ryan did to prepare Hannah for her first day of school so that they can learn how to ask questions of others and build rapport. Role-playing is used extensively at the Farm as an effective training tool, so why not practice it with our kids as well? Just after Ryan's divorce, he regularly stayed with the Bigs in a hotel near their bio-mom's house on nights during the school week so he could have extra time with them. He was working a few hundred miles away at the time, and he put massive mileage on his car during that time driving back and forth to see the kids as much as he could. On those nights in the small Bavarian-style hotel, he and the kids role-played everything from convincing their teacher to give them extra credit opportunities to interacting with law enforcement. The Bigs grew to love these exercises, and it laid the groundwork for their interactions with friends and adults for years to come.

Key Principles to Teach Your Kids About Building Rapport with Others

As you start to role-play and implement these techniques with your kids, here are a couple of things for you to emphasize as you teach them the concept of You Me, Same Same:

1. **They shouldn't pretend to be someone they're not.** Your kids should find a genuine common interest, and if there isn't one, they should try to take a genuine interest in one of the other person's interests. If they don't currently have a particular skill but they're interested in learning, that's perfectly fine and can be a great way to build rapport. That puts the other person in the position of teacher with something they are passionate about. Your kids should do this only if they really are interested in learning the activity. Ryan often

reminds me of when I feigned interest in learning to ski when we met. He's still trying to convince me that it's safe, and I'm still terrified of flying down a mountain at full speed, not to mention the chair lift! Whatever your kids do, they shouldn't pretend to be interested in something they're not.

I'm reminded of the sister in the movie *27 Dresses*, who pretends to be a vegetarian, outdoorsy animal lover to connect with a man. It works for her up to the point of wedding planning, until her sister, played by Katherine Heigl, exposes her at her wedding rehearsal dinner as the true meat-loving, dog-disdaining, indoor woman she is, at which point their relationship crumbles. Likewise, friendships and relationships that are built on dishonesty won't flourish.

2. Help them find what speaks to them. Emphasize to your kids that one of the best ways to make friends is to focus on what they're interested in so that they can meet and befriend people who also enjoy those activities. That's not to say that they shouldn't also strive to have friends who are different from them, but we're focusing on teaching them how to build relationships with commonality as a starting point, emphasizing that people are often more alike than we realize. In order to do this, your kids need to find what truly speaks to them. What's their scuba diving? You can help them find this when you're exploring interests and hobbies with them. It may take years to discover what they really love, and that's okay. It may also change multiple times along the way, and that's okay too.

3. Encourage them to try new things but know when to let it go. It's also important to encourage your kids to try new things, but you should be prepared to allow them to stop doing something you thought they'd enjoy but they don't. For example, Ryan insisted that we encourage the Bigs to try multiple sports, including the ones they really didn't want to try, like cross-country and tennis. His belief, and I agree, is that you don't truly know if you dislike something until you try it. And even though the kids haven't continued with either of those sports, the fact that they've done them, even a little, is just another interest to add to their portfolio on which they can pull from at different points in their life.

4. Open their eyes to the world. We suggest seeking opportunities to introduce your kids to other cultures and worldviews as early as possible, and one way to do that with older kids is through things like daily readings about international current events (as discussed). And for younger kids, you can start to explore the wider world through things like puzzles and even food. For example, we began introducing Ari to the world map and country puzzles before we even started working on the alphabet and shapes with him. We knew that while of course letters and shapes are important, learning geography and about other cultures is just as vital, if not more so, to us. Case in point, one of Gigi's first words was *Africa* (proud mama moment!). Another way to do this early with kids is to introduce them to several different kinds of foods from various parts of the world while they're young. That's not to say that the Littles (and even the Bigs at times) don't enjoy mac and cheese and chicken nuggets like many other American kids! But it also means that if we're having chicken tikka masala for dinner, then that's what's for dinner. We don't entertain requests—or demands, as they often sound like from our tantruming toddlers—to make mac and cheese instead.

The concept of You Me, Same Same is one that if your kids can master it while they're young, it will help them throughout their life and give them an advantage as an adult. At a time when our country often feels more divided than ever, it's important to remember that we're more alike than we realize. Find the common thread. And remember, life is all about relationships.

CHAPTER NINE

THE PEN IS MIGHTIER THAN THE SWORD

How to Communicate Effectively

"Uuuugh, no, Lena, you don't get it." Hannah groaned in frustration. "Look at this paragraph," she continued. Lena sat next to her at the kitchen table, a look of exhaustion and confusion on her face. They had been at it for over an hour, while I sat on the couch in the other room, tuning in and out. I couldn't help but smile.

When I first came downstairs from putting the Littles to bed, I could barely believe my eyes. Hannah? Helping Lena with her paper? It wasn't even four months ago that I was sitting at this same kitchen table helping *Hannah* learn how to write a research paper for the college-level course she was taking as a high school junior. I had experienced those same feelings of frustration when helping Hannah, but I had tried my best to disguise them so she wouldn't pick up on it.

"You should have seen her other draft; it was *so* bad," Hannah said to me when Lena was taking a bathroom break.

"Okay, well, don't tell her that. You need to build her up and give her confidence. Try pointing out the things that she did well in addition to the things that she needs to improve," I told her.

"Okay, but seriously, you should see it. It's so much better now that I've fixed it," she said proudly. In reality, no one could be more proud than I was in this moment. I had spent a significant amount of time over the previous months helping Hannah essentially learn to write. The thing about Hannah is that she's an amazingly creative and descriptive writer. Give her a narrative assignment and she'll blow you away with the story that she paints. When it came to a more formal research paper or something that required analysis and supporting data points, she tended to struggle more. She didn't have the patience or interest in learning and spending the time on correct grammar and punctuation. She also had never had someone sit down with her to teach her in a way that she understood.

After reviewing countless drafts of Hannah's papers, I wasn't pleased just with her ending the fall semester with straight As, I was even more pleased that she hadn't asked me to review her last few papers because she felt comfortable and confident in her own abilities. Seeing her coach Lena, however, brought it to another level. It told me two things: (1) she had truly absorbed the writing lessons I had taught her, and (2) she finally understood how much energy and time I had put in to help her learn, even when it was painfully frustrating, like she was now experiencing firsthand with Lena. It wasn't just rewarding for me because I wanted to see her succeed, like any parent wants for their child. It was especially rewarding because I was able to impart one of my strongest traits, which I fully credit to the CIA—my ability to write well.

Why Writing Matters in Espionage

While it's often the clandestine side of the CIA that is portrayed in Hollywood, one of a spy's most prized, and often overlooked, traits is the ability to write and to do it well. Each analyst who joined the DI went through four months of rigorous analytic training called the Career Analyst Program (CAP), which included writing, briefing, and critical-thinking exercises. In short, I was trained to become a master at communicating. I learned how to synthesize enormous amounts of information and distill it into clear, concise analytic judgments. From there, I learned how to communicate those assessments, whether in written or oral form, in a productive way for others to digest easily. The DI was full of subject-matter experts; we were the people the president relied on to tell him what was going on in the countries for which we were responsible. Analysts often read hundreds, sometimes thousands of intelligence reports coming in from the field each day and used many different analytic techniques to inform their intelligence assessments.

I wrote a variety of intelligence products, including short and long articles for the President's Daily Brief (PDB), a compilation of intelligence assessments delivered to the president and his cabinet; articles for an internal classified platform for the intelligence community called the CIA WIRe; and leadership profiles, biographic and psychological profiles of foreign leaders.

In addition to these types of written assessments, I was at the beck and call of policymakers who had questions about my area of expertise, which came in the form of "taskings" from the seventh floor, the top level of the CIA, where the leadership team resided. The taskings were sometimes immediate questions that needed to be answered in a few hours, or in some instances a few days. I balanced these responsibilities with the requirement to write longer, finished intelligence assessments that had a shelf life of anywhere from three to twelve months or more. These were the papers that I needed to produce in order to be promoted, because they demonstrated my abilities and deep expertise as an analyst.

Between writing PDBs, WIRe articles, and leadership profiles, you can imagine how little time I had left to work on those longer research papers. This essentially meant that any analyst who wanted to get ahead and rise through the ranks had to put in extra time. As a result, I regularly went into the office on weekends, where I was at times the only one in a quiet vault, allowing me to make progress on those papers, inching closer and closer to promotion each time.

The primary goal of all these intelligence assessments as a whole, however, wasn't promotion. The purpose of intelligence analysis was to inform policymaking by helping the US government anticipate threats and seize opportunities.[1] In order to do so, you needed to convey information to the president and senior policymakers in a way that was understandable and easy to digest. These were busy people, so the most important part was to have the "bottom line up front," or BLUF. You had to assume that people might not read your entire article, so you needed to lead with the most important information. Essentially, you needed to learn how to write concisely and communicate well.

Writing wasn't the only way analysts communicated with policymakers; they also gave intelligence briefings, or oral presentations, in person. This meant that in addition to communicating well on paper, you needed to know how to speak clearly and succinctly and be ready to field questions on your area of expertise. Prior to briefings, analysts wrote talking points that were coordinated with their analytic team, which meant even more writing! With this type of demand for an analyst's writing, they become quite prolific writers, accustomed to writing an enormous amount of quality material in a very short time.

This training and experience as an analyst paid off and even gave me a leg up on other operations officers in the field station where Ryan and I found ourselves working together in the latter part of my CIA career. I had some operational training prior to my field assignment, but I didn't have the same lengthy training at the Farm that my DO colleagues had.

They were accustomed to writing cable traffic, which were messages sent to and from CIA Headquarters and the field and between field stations. Operations officers learned how to write cables during their training at the Farm, but the bulk of their training consisted of what you'd consider the spooky spy skills I've mentioned, like how to recruit an asset, surveillance detection, offensive and defensive driving, and weapons training, to name a few. These cables, however, were an integral part of their operations in the field. They're how operations officers documented the progress of their cases for Headquarters, and how they did things like request permission from Headquarters to recruit assets.

In addition to cables, they wrote up the foreign intelligence they collected from their assets in intelligence reports, which then went into the system for analysts back at Headquarters to read and analyze. An operations officer's ability to debrief an asset, find the information that's of interest, and write it up in a clear and concise way is paramount to his or her success on a tour. After all, what good is the recruitment of an asset if you can't extract insightful foreign intelligence from them and write it into an impactful report?

Though I didn't have their same operational training (I

participated in a condensed version of it prior to my deployment), I found it didn't matter for me. In fact, I successfully leveraged my DI analytic skills to outproduce every single officer, with the exception of Ryan, and I became the second-highest intelligence report producer of all time at that particular Station. The rate at which I was accustomed to writing in the DI coupled with my eye for identifying useful intelligence reports were like secret weapons that the operations officers didn't have.

Having experienced both the DI and the DO, I'll readily tell you that I believe the DI is the best. This is a running debate we have in our home, and I find that the kids often side with Ryan. What can I say? Writing and briefing have a tough time competing with the sexier side of espionage. But what about writing for the most powerful leader in the free world? Isn't that pretty damn exciting too? I blame Hollywood. All jokes aside, the communication skills that come with learning to write and speak well transcend all professions, and teaching them to your kids is a gift that will set them up for success in whatever path they take in life.

-RYAN-

ANALYSTS AS FORCE MULTIPLIERS

I'll readily admit that most analysts don't just have an uncanny ability to write well, but they can also write quickly, competently, and fluidly. Thankfully, I was made aware of these traits early on in my career, and I regularly utilized analysts' expertise and writing skills to my advantage. The reality is that analysts can be force multipliers when collecting intelligence. I often leveraged their subject-matter expertise and their writing capabilities to increase the number of intelligence reports I wrote. Most espionage operations are done alone—you and an asset together, with no one else. But when the subject matter was specific or there was potential for collecting more intelligence, I didn't hesitate to bring a subject matter expert along. I often found that the amount of intelligence was increased substantially, and if collecting intelligence is the purpose of everything we do, why not use analysts when possible?

That being said, I would never want to be an analyst. The thought of combing through raw intelligence, writing all day long, and crafting finished intelligence products literally makes me want to crawl into a hole. It's not for everybody, but there are those who love doing this. Christina is one of these people.

Thankfully, she is that same force multiplier when it comes to our parenting, and one of the most critical and useful skills she brings to our family is her analytic writing expertise. Sitting at the table helping the Bigs write their research papers is quite possibly the last thing I'd want to do with them—so I'm thankful I have her to do it instead! And although I know it's sometimes not what Christina wants to be doing late at night after a long day of taking care of the Littles, she dominates it in a way that I know I can't, and I know she still finds joy when she has a reason to dust off those CIA analytic skills.

Now, I know Christina tried to convince you the DI is the best, but remember, just like Jack Ryan was swayed to the dark side, so was Christina in her final three years at the Agency. One of the key differences between her and Jack Ryan, however, is that she was actually trained in field operations—thank goodness. What is extremely unique about Christina, and something I admire, is her ability to combine her book smarts from the DI with the street smarts she learned from the DO. This is rare. She's able to build rapport and trust with the same ease with which she can write a stellar intelligence product. In fact, she was so good in the DO, I'm convinced she never would have returned to the DI if she hadn't left the Agency. I'd argue that Hollywood actually gets it right when it primarily portrays the more exciting side of espionage. The freedom and thrill found in clandestine operations is unrivaled and sure as hell beats sitting at a table outlining a paper!

Technology's Negative Impact on Our Kids' Ability to Communicate

Before we get into the nitty-gritty of writing and briefing skills that you can teach your kids, let's take a minute to talk about technology and how it's changed the way our kids communicate in the world today. We've entered a generation in which kids don't remember or haven't even experienced a world without the internet, email, texting, and livestreams of basically whatever they want to watch, whenever they want to watch it. Gone are the days of stretching the phone cord from the kitchen as far as you can around the corner in order to have some privacy while talking to your bestie. Or what about calling your friend's house and asking, "Hi, is Jenny there?" when her parents answer? Our kids won't have these experiences.

They don't have to deal with the inconvenience and lack of privacy that comes along with landlines, and often there's no phone conversation at all as texting overtakes phone calls as the dominant form of communication in many young people's lives.[2] But what does this mean for their ability to communicate? And what about their social skills as a whole?

Texting can be a fantastic, convenient option for kids and adults. However, it comes with its drawbacks, especially for kids. From a practical standpoint, think about your child's ability to write. If they're writing in short form via text and using autocomplete to help them spell, will they really learn how to use proper grammar and punctuation in the long run?

People can also feel comfortable sharing more with someone via text much earlier than they would on the phone, which could lead to inappropriate conversations or your kids trusting someone too soon. Moreover, people can be much harsher from behind a screen than they are in person or over the phone—the opportunities for bullying via text and on the internet should be a real concern for parents (more on this in chapter 12).

Another concern critics have is that texting doesn't allow for tonal cues, leading to misunderstandings and miscommunication. Kids also use technology as a way to handle awkward or emotionally uncomfortable issues, like breaking up with someone. One high school in Boston actually handed out "Face It, Don't Facebook It," pins during a Boston Public Health Commission etiquette seminar to encourage kids to tackle issues directly, without the buffer of texting or social media. These are skills that we want our kids to have. We need them to be able to communicate with others, even on tough issues—because, let's face it, life can be tough. How will they have successful relationships if they only feel comfortable communicating electronically?

Above all else, the overreliance on texting and instant messaging instead of talking on the phone or in person will almost certainly affect our children's ability to communicate with others. It's become easy, and so common that it feels normal. It's so "normal" that some companies are even hiring consultants to help millennials feel more comfortable making phone calls.[3] You guys, this is a problem. Our kids need to know how to have phone conversations. They need to feel comfortable and confident calling someone. But the reality is that with the help of technology, they begin disengaging from face-to-face interaction daily at a young age.

For example, Lena had a friend over one day, and I noticed as they were out on our sport court playing soccer that they each had an AirPod in to listen to music. I didn't think it was necessary. The activity was soccer—why did they have to have music too? Nonetheless, I bit my tongue and thought it might be fun to play to music while kicking the soccer ball around. An hour later, I found them downstairs at the kitchen table, eating snacks—again, each of them with one AirPod in. They sat and ate without even looking at each other.

"Lena, take the AirPods out. You have a guest," I said.

"She has one in too. We're listening to the same music," she said, as if I must have not noticed.

"I know, but if you want to have a friend over, you should be interacting with each other. Otherwise, what's the point? If you're just going to sit and ignore each other while you listen to music, then she might as well not be here." I immediately regretted the direct, perhaps even harsh way I delivered the message when I saw Lena's face turn red. The reality, though, is that we need to seize these in-person opportunities for our children to have healthy social interactions. They need to connect with one another, without the aid of technology.

Encourage your kids to pick up the phone and call their friends when they're making plans, instead of texting them. Have them call their grandparents or other family members and ask about their day. As a rule, when our kids call someone on the phone or someone calls them, we tell them to ask the person three questions and then tell them three things about themselves sometime during the conversation. This is a great rule of thumb for kids because it helps them to learn how to engage with others through both listening and talking, giving them a tangible and easily attainable goal.

While we can't stop things from happening like voice mail becoming a lost art akin to the telegram, we *can* do things to ensure our kids have opportunities to become excellent communicators.[4]

Key Principles to Teach Your Kids About Effective Writing

Now that we've established the fact that our kids have less reason to use traditional forms of communication in their daily lives due to the role of technology, let's talk about how we can bolster their writing abilities through giving them some practical, useful tools to implement that stem from CIA techniques. You may be wondering: *Won't my kids learn how to write in school?* The answer is yes and no. How many of you have children who do what they need to do to get the good grade? How many of you have kids who aren't even worried about the grade and simply skate by? The question we really want you to think about is this: *How much of what your kids are learning at school about writing is actually preparing them for writing in the real world?*

While our Bigs were in middle school, they learned a specific structure, using terms like CDs and CMs—referring to "concrete detail" and "commentary." It appeared to be an effort to help them outline and structure their papers, but what I found with our kids is that they were so caught up in checking off the boxes the teacher required that they didn't really understand it, nor did they find it helpful. "Do I have enough CMs? What about my CDs?" Quite frankly, it's not a realistic structure that kids will absorb and use later. It's cumbersome and counterintuitive, and it just plain doesn't make sense to them—or me, for that matter!

What I loved about the way the CIA taught writing was how formulaic it was. It broke everything down into a structure with questions for you to answer in your research stage. The best part about this approach was that it could be applied to virtually anything you wrote, whether it was a paper, an email, or a presentation. Hannah has always preferred sitting at a blank screen when she writes and seeing where it takes her; however, she, like others, has found that her method, although perfectly suitable for writing fiction, can be problematic when writing a nonfiction, research paper. It's helpful to at least have your structure and data points outlined before the pen hits the paper, so to speak. I always emphasize to the kids that if they do all the legwork beforehand—that is, research and outline their papers—the actual writing should be the fastest part.

Here are some tips I used in my day-to-day life writing at the CIA that can assist you in teaching your kids to write in a way that is useful and impactful throughout different phases of their lives, whether they're in high school or college, or later as an adult seeking to excel in their career.

1. Formulate a question. Intelligence analysis tradecraft teaches analysts to formulate a robust research question at the start, and it shouldn't be a yes-or-no question. Consider using words like *what* and *how*; for example, "What is the likelihood of postelection violence in country X?" or "How will the COVID-19 pandemic impact African economies?" and if you're feeling less creative, something as simple as "What's up with X?" can even work in a pinch. It's also helpful to use this as a starting point for issues you're trying to understand in everyday life. For example, a question many parents— Ryan and me included—were asking ahead of the new school year in the fall of 2020 was, "How will our school district handle remote learning during the COVID-19 pandemic?" Establishing your question before beginning your research will help you narrow your search and bring in the most useful data.

2. Outline your paper. No, I don't mean outline your sections with roman numerals like you learned (and maybe your kids have also already learned) in school:

I. Introduction
II. Body Paragraph
III. Body Paragraph
IV. Body Paragraph
V. Conclusion.

Instead, I suggest filling in a much more useful outline once you've thoroughly researched your intelligence question and have a good idea of the information that you may include in the paper.

There are six questions or categories you can use to help you organize virtually any paper: What, Why, Impact, Outlook, Implications, and Opportunities. I'll quickly walk you through what this process looks like (don't worry, I'll give some more specific examples later).

- **What is happening?** Describe the current situation in your country or on your topic. Come up with a one-line sentence describing the What.

- **Why (or how) is it happening?** Here's where you explain the motivation behind your What. In some cases, the intelligence question may lend itself to a How for this section instead of a Why.

- **What is the impact of what's happening?** This section can feel like an extension of your What, with the primary difference being that these are other examples of what is *already* happening, rather than the current hook you used in your What section. This section is sometimes dropped in shorter papers.

- **So what? What do you think will happen based on your data?** This is where the analysis comes in. It's also referred to as your Outlook section. You take the What and the Why and tell us what that means. Why should the reader, who in the case of CIA analysts is the president of the United States of America, care about what you're telling them?

- **What are the implications of what's happening?** For CIA analysts, this section refers to the implications to the United States, because as I quickly learned as a CIA analyst, US policymakers don't care what's happening in your country unless there's an implication for our country or our citizens. For your child's research topic, it can be any sort of implication or larger consequences of what they've described as their analytic assessment of what's happened and what is likely to happen.

- **What opportunities exist?** Here is where CIA analysts objectively lay out options that the president may or may not choose to utilize. In your child's research paper, this may be a call to action. If they're writing on a topic like climate change, for example, they may provide a call to action in their final section and provide some ideas for how the reader can take steps to control the effects of climate change.

If your child is having difficulty organizing their paper, you can ask them how they would explain the information to you. I often felt that my briefing skills were stronger than my writing skills, so I found it helpful to think about how I would brief the information. That would then help me formulate a structure for a written form of the same information. Have a discussion with your child, asking the preceding questions. Sometimes it's easier to voice the data that's in their head than to put it on paper. This is especially true for kids who are learning to write this way. When I first introduced this structure to Hannah, we sat and talked through each section together.

3. Organize your data points and decide where you'll put them. This is where you're looking for your facts—the supporting evidence that you can cite. If you're required to include quotes for a research paper, now is the time to gather them. Since you've already done your research and organized your sections, this should be easy, simply dropping them into the section where they need to go. This step can be ongoing—as you continue your research, have a Word document open with your structure, leaving gaps for information in each section. Cut and paste quick facts as you find them, and continue on. Don't forget to include sourcing so you don't have to go back to find it later.

4. Create analytic lead sentences. All CIA assessments have analytic lead sentences in each paragraph, and they call these the "bottom line up front," or BLUF. This refers back to writing for busy people and ensuring everything they need to know is in the first line in case they can't finish reading your paper. In academia, these are often referred to as thesis statements. You may have already done your analytic lead sentences when you outlined your sections, or you have an idea of what they'll look like. It's important to keep in mind, however, that if you write your lead sentences too early—that is, before you've done enough research—you could consciously or subconsciously cherry-pick evidence that supports your claims. This is an example of confirmation bias. For this reason, I find it most helpful to write my lead sentences last so that they are a reflection of what the data points say. This is sometimes referred to as the inverted pyramid.

Here's a fictitious example of what your lead sentences may look like using the structure I've described (I've labeled each section for your convenience, but you wouldn't do that in the actual paper):

WHAT: A government crackdown on opposition supporters in Bergtopia led to violent clashes over the weekend.

WHY: The ruling party is threatened by the opposition's increasing momentum; polls indicate this could be the first change in power since the ruling party took over in 1962.

IMPACT: The government has been intimidating opposition members and blocking voter registration in opposition strongholds.

OUTLOOK/SO WHAT: Tension between the ruling party and opposition almost certainly will intensify in the coming weeks, and it's unlikely either party will accept election results, increasing the likelihood for post-election violence.

IMPLICATIONS: A violent aftermath to the elections jeopardizes the stability of one of the United States' strongest allies and counterterrorism partners in the region.

OPPORTUNITIES: International observers at polling stations monitoring the freedom and fairness of the elections and a swift acknowledgment of election results from the international community may legitimize the election results and decrease the chance for violence.

Your very first BLUF of your paper should be the analytic judgment or thesis for the entire paper. A great way to do that is to combine your What and your Outlook sections and rephrase into one robust BLUF that includes your So What in the very beginning of your paper. In this example, it may look something like this:

Violent clashes between opposition supporters and police forces in Bergtopia over the weekend suggest increasing tension ahead of the presidential election and a likelihood of postelection violence.

I've found that this formulaic approach can be applied to just about any type of paper, from the writing sample I had to produce when applying for my first job outside of the CIA to several of Hannah's first college-level research papers. Encourage your child to think of their sections as answers to those six questions. This can make it easier for them to organize and take it in one section at a time so it's less overwhelming. Don't be discouraged if you have to explain this to your child multiple times. For example, remember my proud mama moment seeing Hannah help Lena at the table? A few months later, I had to sit down with Hannah to go over the sections and walk her through it again. It was as if she hadn't heard it before, #becauseteenagers.

This is an extremely simplified and quick version of a CIA analyst's approach to writing. I could easily devote a whole book to this topic alone! My hope with this section is that it will give you and your kids a new way of looking at structuring papers so that it becomes more manageable to them—and to you, if you are lucky enough to experience the pure joy of sitting with your teenager for hours at the kitchen table, poring over their research paper.

Key Principles to Teach Your Kids About Effective Communication in Any Context

The first thing that might come to mind when you're considering how CIA briefing skills can help your kids may be their public speaking or presentation skills. I'm going to share with you some strategies that will help improve your kids' ability to do those things, but what I really want to drive home is that these are communication skills that will help your kids whether they're talking to one person or a hundred. The following are some of the dos and don'ts I came up with and used to share with junior analysts at the CIA. I've tweaked them to show how these same techniques can be beneficial to your kids.

1. Know your audience. When you're giving any sort of presentation, you want to ensure that you take into consideration your audience. For example, if you're presenting to a room of cybersecurity experts, you probably don't need to explain to them basic terms like *phishing*. If you're giving the same instructions to a group of non-experts, you'll need to offer a bit more foundational information. The same is true for when your kids are giving presentations in class or even talking one-on-one to someone. They shouldn't assume someone has a particular background if they don't know for sure, but they should be careful not to dumb something down for an expert, unintentionally insulting them. That's why it's important that as part of your kids' preparation, they do proper background research of their audience. Part of knowing your audience also means picking up on nonverbal cues that they're providing. If you're giving a presentation and you're noticing people nodding off or checking their phones, try not to be discouraged. Take that as a signal that you should liven it up or speed it up because people are getting antsy.

2. Start and end with a road map. When you begin any sort of speech or presentation, it's good practice to start with a road map. What I mean is, tell your audience exactly what you're going to tell them, in the order you're going tell them. For example: "Today I'm going to talk to you about the recent violent clashes between state-owned police forces and opposition members in Bergtopia and what that means for the upcoming elections. I'll walk you through why the government cracked down on the opposition in this manner and other measures they've taken to intimidate the opposition over the past several months. Lastly, I'll discuss implications and opportunities for the United States to encourage and support free and fair elections in Bergtopia." (Notice how this road map follows the same structure as the written paper.) When you finish the briefing, walk your audience through the road map again, reminding them of what you just told them. This may feel awkward the first few times, but the more your child does it, the more conversational and natural it will feel. It helps the audience stay with you and engaged throughout the presentation. It can also help your child remember what they're going to say by organizing it into sections that they're teeing up for themselves.

3. Give your BLUF. Just like I recommended that your child start their paper with the bottom line up front, they should do the same for their briefing. This is important because if their presentation is cut short for any reason, they've already said the most important part. Once they give the road map, they should give their analytic assessment or BLUF:

> *Violent clashes between opposition supporters and police forces in Bergtopia over the weekend suggest increasing tension ahead of the presidential election and a likelihood of postelection violence.*

4. Learn how to give an elevator brief, and practice regularly. As a CIA analyst preparing for a briefing, you should always have your full briefing planned but also be ready to give an elevator brief in the event your time is cut off because the policymaker's schedule has changed. This is a much shorter version than what you originally planned to say, but it gets across your analytic line and the most important information. You should be able to distill your briefing to what you would share on one short elevator ride—that is, only a few minutes long—hence the name elevator brief. The way we practice this with our kids is through what we call Stressed and Stoked, an exercise I learned from a manager in the private sector. I've heard it called variations like Roses and Thorns and Highs and Lows. At the beginning of every week, we go around the dinner table and each person shares one thing that's causing them stress or concern and one thing that they're excited about. Not only is it a fantastic way to learn what's on your kids' minds or what they're proud of (you may be surprised at what they share!), it's also a great way to practice giving elevator briefs. Give each child no more than two minutes to share to keep it moving and to help them practice being clear and concise.

5. Never discredit yourself. I learned early on at the CIA that you should always act confident, even if you don't feel that way. It may be your first week on the job when you're asked to give an important briefing. Whatever you do, don't start the briefing with "Hi, I'm Christina, I've only been on the account for a week . . ." If you discredit yourself in this way at the beginning of your briefing, you've lost all credibility for the entirety of your presentation. The CIA teaches its analysts that even if you've only just started covering a particular country, you don't point that out. If they ask how long you've been on it, you talk in positives: "I'm part of a team of experts on country X, and I've traveled to the region Y number of times over the past five years." Instead of talking about what expertise and time you *don't* have, talk about what you *do* have. As a woman, and a young woman at that, I found this particularly important for me at the CIA. There were often times that I was briefing military customers who were much older men. When they saw that their briefer was a twenty-one-year-old woman, the look on their faces said it all: They didn't think I was qualified. They didn't want to hear what I had to say. That's when you rely on the expertise you have, and you don't let them shake you. You prove to them that you are qualified by giving a substantive, clear, and concise briefing that shows you're an expert, and by the end of it, there's no question about whether you're qualified, because you clearly are. You can teach your kids this same principle. When they start a briefing or presentation, they should be confident. They've done the research, and they are the experts on their topic.

6. If you don't know something, don't guess or make it up. Nothing hurts credibility, or in your child's case their grade, more than guessing or making up information when they don't know the answer. If their teacher asks them something as a Q&A portion of their presentation and they don't know, they shouldn't be afraid of saying so, and a great way to do that is to follow it up with a fact: "I'm not aware of X, but I do know Y." In some cases, it may even be appropriate to say, "I don't have that answer, but I can get back to you." That may not always fly for a child's assignment, but it's an important lesson for life in general. Generally speaking, you gain credibility when you show candor and initiative to find the correct answers for someone.

7. Be aware of your voice. Lastly, I want to emphasize how important it is for your child to be aware of any filler words they use, like

umm, uh, or *you know,* as well as variations in their voice. For example, some people have a tendency to use uptalk, or upspeak, in which
there is an inflection in their voice, or a rise, at the end of their de-
clarative sentences, making everything sound like a question.
There's also been increasing use of vocal fry, a tendency to draw out
the end of your sentences in a creaky way, due to a lot of celebrities,
like the Kardashians, speaking like this. I'm not saying you should
tell your kids that they can never speak like this—because they
shouldn't have to change who they are—but what I *am* saying is that
they should be aware of it. When they're giving a presentation, they
want to sound authoritative and confident, and when everything
sounds like a question, that makes it difficult. It can also be distract-
ing for some listeners. However, when your kids are hanging out
with friends or in a more casual setting, there's nothing wrong with
any of those voice qualities. Being aware of the different registers
you use with your voice can make your kids more impactful speak-
ers in a variety of settings.

While these aren't the flashy spy skills that will get your kids out of
a dangerous spot, they are the skills that will help them succeed in
school and in just about any career. By teaching them these tools
along with the You Me, Same Same techniques you learned in the
previous chapter and the persuasion skills you'll learn next, you're
setting them up to be master communicators.

CHAPTER TEN

PLANT A SEED

How to (Appropriately) Persuade Others
to Your Way of Thinking

"If you tell Hunter you want cheesecake, he's going to choose something else," Ryan told her. "You need to make him crave cheesecake. Put the idea in his head."

We were headed to my in-laws' to celebrate Hunter's thirteenth birthday for the second time that week, this time with extended family, and planned to make a stop at Costco to pick up a cake along the way. Hunter had already made it clear that he wanted another chocolate cake, much to the disapointment of our oldest daughter, Hannah. Hunter was in the backseat of our Suburban with headphones on, and I listened to Ryan explain the CIA way of persuasion and manipulation to Hannah with the ultimate goal of Hunter choosing her favorite dessert, cheesecake.

Ryan began to teach her some basic techniques and encouraged her to play it cool and let Hunter naturally come to the conclusion himself. He role-played with Hannah a few times to ensure she emphasized certain key words and phrases—one of them being "cheesecake" and another "a cold glass of milk."

As we got closer to Costco, Hunter took off his headphones.

"So what kind of cake are you thinking you want, Hunter?" Ryan asked.

"Chocolate," Hunter said confidently.

"Oh, that sounds good," Hannah said as she carefully started her clandestine op. "Their cakes are really good . . . sometimes they have too much icing, but they're good."

"Oh . . . yeah . . . sometimes they *do* have too much icing," I could hear the seeds of doubt already sown in Hunter's voice— much to my disappointment, because I actually wanted chocolate cake too!

"What other cakes are there?" Hannah asked Hunter. He wasn't sure, so she continued, "I think they also have white cake, apple pie . . . I think they might have cheesecake too. . . . Cheesecake with a cold glass of milk, that sounds good." There was that key phrase Ryan told her to include.

Ryan took Hunter into the store and headed to the back where all the cakes were located. There were so many options, including an enormous chocolate Seahawks-themed cake, which ordinarily would have been a slam dunk, but Hunter slowly walked over to the refrigerated area where the cheesecakes were located and asked Ryan if he thought Grandma and Grandpa had milk at their house.

The girls and I were waiting in the car when we saw Hunter and Ryan walking out of the store and toward our car. Hunter was smiling, and Ryan was smiling even bigger.

In his hands?

A fucking cheesecake.

Plant the Seed

If you're asking someone to betray their country to serve yours, you'd better hope you're convincing. That's why CIA officers undergo extensive training on the art of persuasion. It all starts with You Me, Same Same, and over time, while the CIA operations officer continues to build a relationship of trust with the asset, he or she is also planting seeds along the way. Just like Hannah planted her key phrase, "a cold glass of milk," with Hunter, operations officers do the same with their assets. If the officer plants seeds along the way using key phrases, the asset may even think the clandestine relationship is their idea. Case in point: to this day, Hunter still vehemently believes that buying cheesecake for his birthday was *his* idea.

-RYAN-

THE MISTRESS

While at a diplomatic reception overseas, I struck up a conversation with a foreign diplomat who I later learned had an intimate relationship with a prominent foreign leader of interest to the CIA. After several weeks of meeting with me and discussing a variety of topics, one day she shared with me a political opinion she had about something going on in the world.

"You know, your take is really interesting," I told her. "I think people back in Washington would really like to know this perspective. Would you mind if I shared it with them? Of course, I wouldn't include your name." There were three specific seeds that I was trying to plant here: (1) I let her know that her perspective was important, (2) I made sure she was comfortable with me sharing that information, and (3) I emphasized that I would not be attributing it to her. This last seed was particularly important because it helped the potential asset know from the very beginning that I was protecting her (more about how we protect our assets in chapter 14). All of these seeds were intentional so that once the relationship was further along, I knew she would feel comfortable providing confidential information of which only she was privy by virtue of her position as a foreign diplomat and her romantic relationship with a foreign leader. When you're intentional about the key phrases that you use from the beginning, you're creating a solid foundation for a fruitful clandestine relationship with a recruited asset down the road, which this foreign diplomat indeed turned out to be for me.

The art of persuasion at the CIA is about more than planting seeds, though. It has to do with understanding a person's motivations, or what makes them tick, and their vulnerabilities. This time before recruitment is called development, and it's during this period that the operations officer does something called asset validation, which basically amounts to various operational tests to confirm that the asset is the person he claims to be and the information he is sharing is factual. In addition to evaluating the information, the operations officer is constantly assessing the person psychologically to understand him better and decide the best way to pitch him for recruitment—that is, a formal clandestine relationship with the CIA.

In order to recruit assets, it's critical to understand what motivates them because you can use that information to help you craft the perfect recruitment proposal. For example, some may be motivated to work with the CIA because they have financial hardship; others may want to share information out of respect for the United States or a sense of patriotism. During my rotation with the DO, I approached a prominent businessman with access to foreign intelligence in a sub-Saharan African country and several other high-priority countries around the world by nature of his professional position. Prior to making initial contact, I conducted thorough background research and learned that his parents had been killed in a terrorist attack when he was just a young boy. At the time, I didn't know the extent to which that event had impacted him, but I made an assumption that it had in some way. We met regularly, and I continued to develop my relationship with him, often using You Me, Same Same about Africa as a way to connect with him. I knew he had a soft spot for the time he had spent there, as evidenced by the artifacts that hung on his office walls and around his neck. Throughout the development stage, I learned that the terrorist attack didn't just impact his life, it shaped—or reshaped, as the case turned out to be—the course of his adult life. And ultimately, it became his primary reason for providing me with intelligence.

When the relationship between the CIA and an asset reaches the point of recruitment, it shouldn't be a surprise to the asset. If an operations officer has done their job well, the asset might say, "Why did it take you so long to ask? I would have said yes months ago." The answer to this is due to a few factors—one is that recruitment, like anything in the federal government, requires a bureaucratic process with sign-offs from multiple stakeholders, so it never happens as quickly as you'd like. The main reason, however, is that a pitch for recruitment has to be a sure thing. The last thing you want is to pitch someone who says no and then turns you in to his government, resulting in your expulsion from the country—so you'd better be pretty damn sure you're convincing.

In fact, when asset development and recruitment is done correctly, the bond created between the operations officer and the asset can last decades. While CIA officers do not maintain contact with their assets once they turn them over to the next officer, it's not unusual for the asset to speak fondly of this very first handling officer who recruited him. In fact, Ryan once had an asset who had been on the books for nearly thirty years who still reminisced about the early days with the officer who recruited him.

Wait a Minute . . . How Many Times Have I "Chosen Cheesecake"?

Seeing Ryan in action with Hannah that day on the way to pick up Hunter's birthday cake, I couldn't help but look back on my own conversations with him and wonder how many times he had planted seeds with me so that I would unknowingly suggest his idea as my own. I knew operations officers were persuasive, but I thought I would recognize it when it happened to me. What I found, though, was that if they were good at their job, I wouldn't.

My mind listed off choices I had made since meeting Ryan that I knew weren't initially my idea, but I *had* made the call. First, there was the Toyota FJ Cruiser I bought myself so that I could more easily drive over the mountain pass to see Ryan every weekend early in our relationship. The only vehicles I had driven prior to that were small sedans. But this was a practical decision based on roads and safety, right? Then there was our short engagement. I *had* always planned on being engaged a full year, but why wait when you know who you want to marry . . . right? And then there was . . . oh yes . . . our dog.

We were less than a year into our marriage when Ryan received a call from a dog breeder with whom he had been in touch for years. Norah was from what was then known as Rhodesia—now Zimbabwe—and was one of the oldest Rhodesian ridgeback breeders in the world. One of Ryan's deal breakers when we became engaged was that he would never marry someone who wouldn't agree to one day have a Rhodesian ridgeback. Getting a dog, and this breed in particular, was a promise he had made to his kids. I shrugged my shoulders at the time and said sure—assuming I'd be able to talk him into a much smaller, fluffier dog with some variation of -*poo* or -*doodle* in it. I'd grown up with two cats, and I had always been afraid of large dogs. I later learned that when Ryan had a deal breaker, there was no changing it. And because Ryan never breaks promises to the kids, a Rhodesian ridgeback it would be—but later. Much later. After we had a baby, of course. To which Ryan agreed.

"Well, she has one for us, if we want it." Ryan said cryptically as he came back to our table at IHOP. He was careful not to mention the word *puppy*, for fear of getting the kids' hopes up. He knew getting one this early in our marriage wasn't the plan.

"Umm, we're a few years too early, right? I mean, we're not even trying for a you-know-what yet," I said, careful not to mention the word *baby* in front of the kids either, although they seemed fully engrossed in deciding which variation of stuffed French toast they would choose.

"This is her last litter," he mouthed to me from across the table.

I knew what that meant. Ryan had been hoping to get a puppy from Norah for years, but his overseas lifestyle with the CIA and a period of instability before and after his divorce made it tricky. He had already been planting seeds not so subtly with me for the previous two years, championing what an amazing breed these former lion-hunting dogs were. He told me how it was the most popular breed for CIA officers, which clearly meant we were destined for one too, right? He told me how they were just as content lounging about the house as they were running for miles, because it was most important for them to be near their owners. They would only bark if there was a reason to do so and were protective of both their owners and their property. More than anything, he told me, they were family dogs and loved kids.

Even so, I still wasn't convinced and remained terrified of owning a dog that was considered a large breed, nudging awfully close to *giant*, but I started researching them nonetheless. I found conflicting information—some that confirmed what Ryan had told me and then of course horror stories of ill-behaved Rhodesian ridgebacks that confirmed my greatest fears. It seemed you could find just about whatever information you were looking for if you searched just right. We decided to make a trip forty minutes north to Norah's house so I could meet the pups myself.

"I don't usually let people visit the pups this early, you know," Norah said.

"Thanks for making an exception for us," I said.

She was a tough woman to read. She had grown up on a farm in Rhodesia, and her no-nonsense personality was likely a result of her rugged upbringing in the remote parts of southern Africa. She could be curt but not toward Ryan. Somehow, over the years of talking to her on the phone whenever she was preparing for a new litter, Ryan had, of course, won her over. What they had in common God only knew, but he had obviously managed to You Me, Same Same this woman up the ying-yang, because she was his biggest fan. Her feelings toward me were indifferent at best; after all, I was questioning her most beloved breed, which also happened to be her life's purpose. It was safe to say I wasn't winning her over.

She had told us prior to the visit that under no circumstances would we be allowed to touch the puppies, so you can imagine my surprise when she offered to let us hold the pup she had chosen for us. He fit into the palm of my hand, and it was hard for me to imagine how something so small, sweet, and helpless could ever grow to be a scary, ferocious dog, especially if we trained him as early as eight weeks old, when Norah said we'd be getting him, if we chose to go through with it.

Ryan had done all the legwork, and now all he had to do was plant a few more seeds and then let me take it from there.

"I mean, Norah *could* change her mind and have another litter down the road, but this might be our last chance to have one of hers," he said to me on our drive back home that evening.

"She's been doing this for decades and knows what she's doing," he continued. "So we know we'd be getting an amazing dog with a good temperament." And then he added the clincher: "It could also be good protection for you at home when I'm traveling."

"Uh-huh," I said, trying to sound unconvinced.

"But it's your decision, sweetie. If you're not ready, then we'll just find a breeder when we *are* ready," he said reassuringly.

He put the decision squarely in my lap. The words "last chance" kept ringing in my ears. And more loudly than that, "protection." Ryan was traveling frequently during this time, and I didn't like being alone in our new home. Remember what I said about understanding someone's motivations? He knew I worried about being safe when alone. We weren't even trying to get pregnant yet, I thought to myself. But if we were going to get a puppy, he was right that we should get one from a reputable breeder. Norah was one of the best—maybe even *the* best. And suddenly, as if I had been in agreement all along, I couldn't think of a good reason why we shouldn't say yes.

There was no doubt about it; Ryan was good. He knew when to push a little and when to let things do what he calls "float." He planted the seeds but let me make the call. I had no one to blame but myself if it went tits up, although I knew that wouldn't entirely be true. I hadn't forgotten that getting the dog was his idea in the first place.

But it wasn't a mistake.

I fell in love with that dog from the second I held him in the palm of my hand. I named him Duma, Swahili for "cheetah" and Zulu for "thunder." And to get my buy-in even more, Ryan suggested we train him with Swahili commands, even though I was the only one in the family who spoke it.

"We'll learn," he told me as we all packed into the car to pick him up late one evening after work. I took photos with Duma each week, like a proud mama placing her human baby next to blocks with ages on them each month, but he quickly grew too large for me to hold. I had gone from cat lover to dog lover and didn't look back. For a time before Ari was born, I threw all my maternal desires (which were often amplified by raising three kids who I was keenly aware already had a mom of their own) into Duma.

Quiet, protective, loving Duma.

When Ari was born, I went through a phase when I didn't have as much time for Duma; he noticed, and I was furious when he once snuck up to the nursery to revenge-pee on the rug. That got my attention, all right! We got past that phase, though, and before I knew it, one-year-old Ari was crawling all over him and using him as a backrest while he drank milk from his sippy cup. It turned out everything Ryan had told me was right. Duma would run and play at the dog park all day long if we'd let him, but he'd also happily sit at our feet, his back to the couch so the front door was always in his line of sight. He rarely barked—in fact, he was an excellent judge of character, only ever showing aggression toward two people in particular. One was a neighbor we didn't trust, and the second was a worker who we later learned was a two-time convicted felon, who had since turned his life around (although Duma clearly wasn't convinced he had). Above all, Duma was the perfect combination of formidable protector and loving companion to the kids . . . and to me.

Devastatingly, Duma died suddenly and unexpectedly from a rare form of cancer just after his third birthday. We now have two more Rhodesian ridgebacks, so I guess you can say those seeds Ryan planted really took root. Oh, and spoiler alert, these dogs are also from Norah. As it turned out, she wasn't done breeding. And now that I was a true convert to Rhodesian ridgebacks, she couldn't be more proud of me; I had finally won her over.

But Why Is Covert Persuasion a Useful Skill for Kids to Have?

Puppies and cheesecake aside, I was having difficulty wrapping my head around why we'd want to teach our kids how to influence others in the same way CIA officers did. My mind immediately went back to some of those less genuine operations officers making attempts at You Me, Same Same, and I couldn't help but roll my eyes. The last thing I wanted was to raise a mini ops officer trying to smooth-talk his way out of every situation. I was even more perturbed because I hadn't wanted cheesecake that day; I'd wanted chocolate. Ryan's attempts at teaching life skills were putting a serious cramp in my dessert cravings!

One of my biggest hang-ups with the idea of teaching kids to be persuasive was that my mind immediately went to negative places like imagining ways our kids could manipulate us into thinking they're staying the night at a friend's house when they're actually at an unsupervised late-night party, for example. But wait a minute, what if they could learn how to persuade others *without* manipulation or deceit? And more important, what if they used these powers of persuasion for good? After all, Ryan convincing me to get Duma had brought us more joy than anything. I wondered how these skills could help our kids get what they wanted and needed out of life. Examples immediately came to mind: talking your teacher into giving you extra-credit opportunities, persuading classmates to vote for you for a student government position, and a real-life example that we experienced with Lena—convincing a coach to give you back your playing position.

Lena's always been gifted at sports. She possesses the natural talent coupled with the drive to continue to improve and learn, making her the ultimate threat on the softball field, in particular. During her seventh-grade year, there was another player, whom we'll call Kate, who was disappointed when Lena beat her out for the position of shortstop. In addition to school softball, Lena played on a recreational team, which Kate's mother coached. Kate regularly played shortstop for those games, and Lena was bumped to other positions, despite it being clear to us and other parents of players on the team that Lena was the stronger shortstop. When school tryouts came around, and when faced with an unbiased coach, Lena earned the position of shortstop. Kate immediately approached Lena with bullying remarks about how Lena "stole her position," and the like. Within days, Lena overheard at school one morning that Kate's mom had contacted the coach to complain about Kate's playing position. At her softball game that afternoon, the coach put Lena in a different position, and you guessed it, Kate played shortstop.

When Lena came home that evening and explained to us what she believed had happened, I had to hold back from emailing the coach immediately. I was furious. How dare they take away Lena's hard-earned position to appease a whiny, overbearing parent? Instead, Ryan took a breath and immediately went into action.

"Here's what you need to do, Lena. Tomorrow morning, I want you to talk to your coach as soon as you get to school," he said. Lena's coach was also her language arts teacher. Ryan went on to teach Lena how to persuade her coach to give her back her position, without even mentioning her knowledge of Kate's mom calling him or Kate's attitude toward Lena's success.

"What do I even say to him?" Lena asked.

"You tell him how hard you've worked for the position. You say that you believe you're the best player for that position. And then you politely request to have your position back, based solely on your merits. You don't need to say a thing about Kate. He'll understand. And when you say that you're the best player, he won't be able to deny it. I know your coach, and I know he gets it. Anyone can be intimidated by a helicopter mom, though, so I also understand why he did what he did to appease her. But at the end of the day, he knows that the right thing to do is to give the position to the better-qualified player who has worked the hardest, and that's you. You can do this, Lena."

"Okay, I'll do it," she said confidently. Ryan went on to role-play with Lena in the same way he's always done to help prepare the kids for various scenarios, and when they finished, he made sure she committed to having the conversation with her coach, even if it felt uncomfortable.

"Promise me you'll talk to him?" Ryan asked.

"I promise," Lena agreed.

We knew that with a little guidance and preparation from us, Lena had the tools and ability to convince her coach based on her own merits alone, without naming names or making it petty, and most important, without direct intervention from us. And when she used the words "I promise," we knew she'd follow through. (You'll learn more about our family's stance on promises in chapter 14.)

Setting Your Kids Up for Life

Persuasion isn't just a skill that your kids can use now; it's a skill that translates into adulthood and can set them up for getting the most out of their professional and personal lives, helping them with every-thing from promotions to getting the girl or boy. For example, think about how many times you've had to use persuasion in a professional setting. Perhaps you've had to help build consensus among your team. Or maybe you disagreed with another person's point of view and wanted to suggest an alternative way of thinking. Knowing how to subtly and diplomatically build a convincing case can be invalu-able, particularly as a woman in a male-dominated field, as I learned when I worked at one of the largest tech companies following my CIA career.

During my time working in information security at this big-tech giant, I can count on one hand the number of times I ran into another woman in the bathroom. Over a period of two years! Meanwhile, there was almost always a line to the men's room; it was like living in an alternate universe where men finally learned what it was like to wait to pee.

"So you've been here a month, and it's obvious you're not happy," my manager told me one day on our walk back to his office. We had just finished a team meeting, where I had gotten into what I believed was a professional, albeit lively debate with my male teammate about his approach.

"What makes you say that?" I asked, unsure of what he meant.

"You were really passionate and aggressive in there," he said.

"Because I disagreed? Well, I guess you can say I feel strongly about it, but I don't think I was any more aggressive than John was," I said as matter-of-factly as I could, lest he call me "emotional" next. I was doubtful he had ever used the words *passionate* or *aggressive* to describe any ambitious high-powered male in the office, but as a woman in tech, I was starting with the deck stacked against me. That meant I needed to use my powers of persuasion better next time. I didn't have the luxury of aggressively debating in the same way the men did.

Coming from the CIA, I was accustomed to having lively analytic debates with both men and women, and gender inequality was never an issue I encountered, thankfully. I had mistakenly leaned solely on my analytic tradecraft in this meeting, and I realized that from then on, I needed to leverage not just my analytic training, but my time in the DO as well. I needed to come to each meeting armed to the teeth with data points, as well as a convincing argument and demeanor. I needed to play the game.

Now, we can discuss whether this type of work environment is right. *It's not.* Or whether it's toxic. *It is.* But the point is, I realized I had the skills to get my message across, even in this chauvinistic environment. Over the next several months, I spent more time building relationships of trust with my new, mostly male colleagues, particularly the one with whom I had sparred, utilizing what I knew from the CIA's You Me, Same Same approach. We connected over everything from the restoration of his Craftsman home to his large-breed dog. As I spent more time creating rapport with him, I began to seed some of the ideas I had for updating the program. Not surprisingly, our future meetings were much less tense and, dare I say, more productive. These persuasion skills work. And if this is the case, then why not equip our kids with this skill set so that they too are set up for success in their professional adult lives?

Key Principles to Teach Your Kids About Positive Persuasion

It's important that you realize that your kids' ability to persuade others to their way of thinking doesn't happen in isolation; this skill builds on other CIA techniques, like You Me, Same Same, for example. It's only after your kids have learned to build rapport through shared interests that they'll have an opportunity to even *attempt* to influence someone. Here are some of the key takeaways that you can use to help your kids become just as persuasive as the world's best spies:

1. Role-play with your kids. Just like Ryan and Lena role-played her future conversation with her coach, you can do the same for your kids. It's one thing to talk to your kids about what they can say to someone to be persuasive; it's another thing to actually act it out with them. This may feel uncomfortable or silly to them (and maybe even you!) the first few times, but the more you do it, the more natural it will feel to them and to you. And as with everything we've discussed, do your best to make it fun.

2. Let them practice in a safe space. Give your kids opportunities to practice their persuasive skills at home in a fun, safe way so that they can learn what it's like to succeed and to fail. You can discuss their mistakes, and it can become a lesson for multiple kids at once. For example, the cheesecake story lives on in infamy in our house, and not only because Hunter still thinks it was his idea but also because it was a lesson for all three of the Bigs—for Hannah, who did the persuading; for Hunter, who was influenced; and for Lena, who observed. Observing helps them learn how to recognize when someone may be attempting to influence them, which is arguably just as important as doing the convincing themselves.

3. Give them the independence to practice in real life. It can be tempting to step in for our children when we feel they've been wronged, but before you do so, take a step back and consider whether this could be a good opportunity for your child to practice their persuasion skills. For example, when Lena lost her position on the softball field, we saw that as an opportunity for her to make an attempt to sway her coach back to her side. Of course, if this were a more serious matter, we would have intervened, but often, our kids are fully capable of resolving matters themselves, just as Lena did in this instance.

The more your kids practice this skill set with you, the better at it they'll get. And when your kids have mastered this skill, the world is theirs. Just ensure you guide them to use their powers for good.

CHAPTER ELEVEN

CONSIDER THE SOURCE

How to Vet Information You Gather
(and Make Good Choices)

"Who ate the chocolate doughnut?" I asked, trying to keep my cool. Ryan and I had been married for nearly two years at this point, and it was common knowledge that the only type of doughnut I ate was made of chocolate cake, while the rest of the family ate original glazed. Admittedly, sharing a home with three kids after not having had roommates for nearly ten years could be trying for me at times. Perhaps it sounded silly, but having to share my food was (and still is) one of my biggest pet peeves, especially when I was pregnant, like I was at this time.

"It wasn't me!" Hannah was quick to respond. As the oldest and most rule abiding of the three Bigs, she was always quick to deny an accusation when it wasn't her. It was a sweet trait, but best of all, it made it rather obvious when it *was* her.

"I don't know," Hunter said with a shoulder shrug.

"I didn't do it," said Lena.

"Listen, I know that one of you isn't telling the truth right now. I'll find out who it was, so you might as well go ahead and tell me," Ryan said, remaining calm but firm.

After much prodding, Hunter finally came clean.

"Okay, it was me, Dad. Sorry!" he said.

All the while, Ryan and I couldn't help but notice how quiet Lena had been throughout the conversation. He took her aside and asked her again.

"It was you too, wasn't it?" he said.

"Yeah," she said, her eyes fixed to the floor.

Ryan had an uncanny ability to know when the Bigs were lying, and his knack for drawing the truth out of them was just as impressive.

"You guys aren't in trouble because you ate a doughnut that wasn't yours, although that's not very considerate; you're in trouble for not telling us the truth. And, Lena, you were going to let your brother take the fall for you!" As it turned out, Hunter had taken a piece of the doughnut, but Lena had come by and finished the whole thing without Hunter ever knowing. When he confessed, she thought it convenient to let him take the fall for the whole incident. After all, why come forward when there was already someone to blame?

This event became known as the Great Doughnut Incident of 2016, and while we all still get a laugh about how Lena left her brother out in the cold, it serves as an important lesson for the Bigs. We explained to them that it wasn't about the doughnut. It was never about the doughnut. Okay, that's not entirely true. I really wanted that chocolate doughnut. But really, it was about the importance of understanding there are multiple sides to every story—and not everyone is always truthful. There was Hunter's version, Lena's version, and then there was what *really* happened.

When There's More Than a Doughnut at Stake

At the CIA, the stakes are much higher than Mom's chocolate doughnut getting eaten, although I do admit to morphing into Momzilla at times when I'm feeling hangry. Indeed, proper vetting and corroborating of information can mean the difference between life and death. Operations officers continually vet their assets to make sure their intelligence is factual and accurate. Analysts are also an important part of this process because they look at intelligence reports from multiple sources, and when doing so they weigh information using various analytic techniques to make judgments. As an analyst, I combed through hundreds of reports on a daily basis and made determinations on whether the reporting was credible. It was the DO's job to describe the source's reliability in each report, but as an analyst and subject matter expert, I was trained in understanding mind-sets and biases and how they can impact the reporting.

It's also important that analysts understand how to objectively weigh data and evidence without letting any of their own mind-sets and biases influence the analysis. I was trained to recognize my own biases when weighing information, through several analytic exercises that used data-driven approaches. Once analysts examine all of the intelligence, they form what is called an "analytic line" on an issue or topic, which becomes the Agency's analytic assessment. They then present the analysis to the president and other policymakers so that they can make an informed decision. These assessments are expected to be objective, and under no circumstances should they be policy prescriptive, although US policy decisions—for example, whether to provide US military support to a country in need or withdraw US personnel amid an outbreak of instability in a foreign country—are often made as a result of them, so it's critical that the intelligence is accurate.

While it's important to understand an asset's motivations when persuading them to agree to a clandestine relationship, it's just as important to continue to assess their motivations and understand how those motivations may influence their decisions over time. For example, if an asset is financially motivated and has come to rely on the money we give him in exchange for intelligence, what would he do if his access to intelligence dried up? Is your relationship good enough that he would feel comfortable telling you that he no longer has intelligence to offer you? Have you assessed his character enough to know if he's someone who may begin fabricating information? How will you know if that's happening?

Prior to Ryan and me getting married, we were fortunate to work on a case together. While operations officers generally don't work in tandem, I was technically still an analyst and subject matter expert—despite being on a field operational assignment—so when Ryan recruited an asset with access to an African leader, it only made sense to bring me onto the case as a force multiplier.

Our asset was regularly traveling back and forth to a country of interest in sub-Saharan Africa and claimed access to the country's prime minister. We hadn't gotten a substantial amount of intelligence from him yet, and we were anxious for his next trip to the continent, during which, he said, he would have a personal meeting with the leader. We provided money for him to purchase a gift for the prime minister as a kind gesture. Our only ask was that he provide a receipt after he purchased what he felt was culturally appropriate.

Weeks later when I met him for a trip debriefing, I asked what he'd decided to purchase the prime minister.

"A pair of shoes," he said.

"Oh really, a pair of shoes? How did you know what size shoe he wears?" I asked.

"Size ten. All men from my country wear a size ten. I wear a size ten, my twin brother wears a size ten, everyone wears a size ten!" he proclaimed.

"Oh, I see," I said, trying to disguise my skepticism. Of course his *twin* brother wore the same size as he did! But everyone else in the country? Doubtful. He didn't really think I was that dumb, did he?

I described the conversation to Ryan when I got back to the office—he'd had another asset meeting, so I had gone to this one solo.

"Oh, Jesus," Ryan said, trying not to laugh. "That's the most ridiculous thing I've ever heard. He bought *himself* a pair of shoes."

"Oh man, you're right," I said.

As someone who had left his home country seeking success in another country, it was probably important to our asset to look well dressed and successful when he returned there. If he had shared this desire with us, we likely would have provided him the money he needed to purchase the shoes for himself. The fact that he'd hidden this information from us, however, called into question his reliability as a source. As Ryan dug further, we learned that the shoes weren't the only thing he was lying to us about. In the end, we decided the asset had character issues and couldn't be trusted to give us accurate, truthful information, so we terminated the clandestine relationship. Even when a clandestine relationship ends, CIA officers follow the rule of the three Fs: firm, final, and friendly. Firm so that the asset understands there's no amount of convincing that will change the officer's mind, final because we want it to be crystal clear that the relationship is over, and friendly because we never know when we may need to reach out to that person again, if ever.

Thankfully, what our asset was lying about wasn't life-or-death. But sometimes it is. Take the Khost bombing in Afghanistan in 2009, for example. When a CIA asset arrived at Camp Chapman for a debriefing on December 30, he detonated a suicide vest after exiting his vehicle, killing seven CIA officers. It turned out he wasn't the prized asset who had penetrated al-Qaeda's upper echelons, like they believed. He was a triple agent who had come there intending to kill as many CIA officers as possible.[1]

-RYAN-

THE FABRICATOR

I once had an asset turned over to me who was allegedly a member of a terrorist cell. He provided regular intelligence, and while it was always just enough information to make it interesting, it was never actionable. This was an asset I had been running for at least a year, and over time, I began to get the sense that he was either embellishing his access, or worse, he was fabricating the information in exchange for money. I decided to do an operational test to verify that he was who he said he was and that the information he was providing was true. There are a variety of ways to do these sorts of tests, including polygraphs, psychological profiling, and other means. I decided that I would create false intelligence and see if the asset would bite.

Just before a planned presidential visit to our region, I asked my asset to keep his eyes and ears open for any potential threats against the US president. I also told him that we had received intelligence from separate channels that indicated there was going to be a terrorist strike using helicopters for a very specific coordinated attack. This was false information I had created as a way to test the veracity of the asset's reporting, and while it sounded plausible to the asset, the threat I described was completely unrealistic. I had decided that if the asset came to our next meeting with corroborating information on the fictitious threat, I would slowly terminate the clandestine relationship over the coming months. If he came back and said he had heard nothing about it, that meant he passed this ops test, and I would continue the relationship. Unfortunately, at our next meeting, he came back with a wealth of information on this very specific helicopter attack, and again, it was enough information to make it interesting without being actionable. My suspicions were confirmed; he was a fabricator.

Knowing Whom or What to Believe

In the same way that assets may decide to lie, fabricate intelligence, or skew information, we expect our kids to encounter versions of this in their daily lives from people ranging from acquaintances to friends and even teachers. And if the Great Doughnut Incident of 2016 tells us anything, they'll likely even do it themselves. It's important that we discuss with them how to weigh evidence and consider mind-sets and biases. They need to understand that everyone is bringing their own bias to a situation, and learning what drives that person will help us understand their view of the world. One of the best ways to do this is for your kids to utilize the You Me, Same Same approach we discussed earlier. When they make an effort to connect with someone using that person's interests and frame of reference, this can help them understand the other person's perspective.

We want our kids to be open-minded, seeking to understand multiple perspectives. In order to help them do so, we recommend encouraging your kids to hear multiple sides of a story before deciding their truth. That means if there's a conflict between friends, we want them to strive not to take sides until they hear each person's version of what happened. They should also make every effort to hear things from the original source whenever possible, understanding that the game of telephone isn't just a game. When information goes through multiple people, it often changes along the way, and everything they hear isn't always true. In fact, there's a term for information that is obtained unofficially through the halls at the CIA; it's called RUMINT, which is short for "rumor intelligence." And it's up to Agency officers to determine what they do or don't believe about their colleagues.

Similarly, we want to ensure that our kids are prepared to make these determinations. Hunter experienced this when a friend of his was accused of sending offensive text messages to another student. Hunter, instead of believing what he had heard from other students, went straight to the original source and asked her. When he heard her version, he was able to make a decision based on all the information he had as to who was telling the truth. It helped that Hunter also knew this friend's character and realized that this accusation wasn't in line with the person he had known and been friends with for years. That's not to say that people never make decisions that are out of character—because that can certainly happen—but Hunter treated that as one data point in all the evidence he was weighing to determine the truth. It later came to light that, just as Hunter had determined, she hadn't sent the texts, and while others were shocked to learn that what they had believed all along wasn't true, Hunter was thankful to have sought out more information from the original source. Sometimes in these scenarios, it can be even more difficult when the person your kids are friends with *has* done something that's out of character or something disappointing. Even so, it's important that we teach our kids to strive to be as objective as possible and let the data drive their decision. The person's character can be a data point, but it shouldn't cloud their judgment or override any other equally important data points.

In addition to maintaining objectivity while collecting more information, it's also important that we teach our kids to be willing to change their minds. We don't want them to hold on to a viewpoint even in the face of mounting evidence that tells them otherwise. They need to be able to take in that new evidence and make a sound decision, even if it means changing their mind on something about which they once felt strongly. They may not always learn conflicting information that tells them their viewpoint is incorrect—rather, your kids may simply encounter a different perspective. And in cases like this, we want them to be willing to try something new and understand that their way isn't the only way.

Perhaps the best example of this is my journey to understanding Ryan's parenting style. There were many times when I could have been closed off and shut down some of his methods; indeed, several of them initially gave me pause. After all, we were coming at parenting from two very different perspectives—him as someone who had grown up in the much more adventurous, outdoorsy Pacific Northwest and having actually parented three kids for nearly ten years, and me as a Midwestern girl with no parenting experience apart from what I knew from my own cookie-cutter suburban childhood. It was the relationship of trust that Ryan and I formed with each other, however, that led me to open up and consider that while he was doing things differently than I had envisioned one day doing as a parent, that didn't necessarily mean he was wrong. What I found over time was that his ways weren't just different, in many cases they were better, and observing the Bigs was certainly a testament to this. And if I had to guess, I'd say this was likely another example of Ryan using You Me, Same Same without my even realizing it! Once he had established a solid relationship with me, he could explain the reasoning behind his various approaches in a way that resonated with me, taking into account my upbringing, values, and interests.

Similarly, we want our kids to be able to recognize when there are different, sometimes better ways of doing things. When Ari was three years old, he learned the concept that "people do things differently" from an episode of *Daniel Tiger's Neighborhood* on PBS. Because he often viewed the world in very literal terms, like many toddlers do, he took this concept and ran with it. Even when I pointed out that his shoes were on the wrong feet, he responded, "People like things different ways, Mommy!" He had taken to using Daniel Tiger's lesson to defend any way he had chosen to do something—even if it was the objectively wrong way. At the same time, I often heard him describing things his younger sister did in an understanding way, saying things like, "Oh, Gigi is wearing the hat backwards. That's okay, Mommy. People like different things," which was exactly the kind of thing I wanted to hear from him.

Somewhere along the way though, kids—and even adults—can lose this trait of understanding there are different viewpoints.

Indeed, many of us will wear our shoes on the wrong feet if it means proving that we're right. But we want our kids to change their minds when they learn new information that tells them otherwise, and we don't want them to be afraid of admitting they were wrong about something. One of the best ways to teach them this is to model it for them. Have you changed the way you usually do something because you found a better way? It can be something simple, like the way you've been cutting their apples. Share that with them. Did you think something was true until you read more and learned the opposite? Use that as an example to teach them. One of the most powerful lessons for kids is when parents can admit they're wrong, because, as they'll someday learn firsthand, even adults don't have it all figured out.

It's Okay to Question What Adults Tell You

Just like we want our kids to question authority figures in emergency situations, they should also become comfortable questioning people in positions of authority who are teaching them or giving them information in regular, day-to-day scenarios. This doesn't mean they should directly question or critique their teachers in front of the class about what they're teaching, or anything that extreme. What I mean is that they shouldn't take everything that their teachers, religious leaders, coaches, and quite frankly, even their parents tell them as truth. The teacher or leader may be sharing an opinion or their interpretation of something, and in some cases, they may not explicitly state that it's their opinion, and kids could walk away believing it's factual. For example, one of the Bigs was learning about immigration in class, and the teacher did a poor job at disguising his own opinion on the issue. Thankfully, our child was able to differentiate this opinion from fact, but that may not always be the case. Sometimes it's much more veiled, and many children expect that their teachers are teaching only facts. But if something they're being taught doesn't sound right or true to them for whatever reason, they should seek out more information. We want them to be empowered by the overwhelming access to information that we didn't have as kids—they can easily research facts and find alternative perspectives to come to their own informed perspective. People can have their own agendas, and sometimes those agendas are hidden, so it's important that your kids understand how to examine statements they hear with a critical eye—respectfully, of course.

Similarly, your kids should understand that each news source has its own political bias. There may be a news source you gravitate to that's in line with your political beliefs, and that's certainly okay. However, I'd challenge you to introduce your kids to that source *and* other sources that aren't your favorites or go-tos. Teach them to consult multiple sources, and as an exercise, you can choose a news topic and print out articles from multiple sources to show them how the same topic has been portrayed differently in the news. Or in some instances, you may be able to flip through the channels on your television to demonstrate a major story that's breaking news on virtually every news outlet yet mysteriously not given any coverage on a select few other networks.

Learning How to Read Body Language

One of the reasons why we knew our African asset was lying about the shoes wasn't just because it didn't make sense that every man in an entire country wore the same size. It also had a lot to do with his body language. Research indicates that 80 percent of communication is done nonverbally, and specifically, more than 50 percent of communication is through body language.[2] For example, when people look away or to the side when they're talking to you or give very little eye contact, it can be because they're nervous, but often there's another reason. One of our daughters, for example, has had her own "tell" since she was much younger. When she isn't telling the truth or she's nervous or about to cry, her eyes blink about three times as much as they would normally. In fact, each of our kids has their very own tell, which is why when we want to know who did something and no one is fessing up, Ryan always asks each of them face-to-face. We immediately know the answer, before they even say anything. Sometimes they own up to it, and sometimes they don't, but we always know the truth by their faces.

I'm not telling you this so that you can become a human lie detector to determine when your kids aren't telling you the truth. In fact, I'd suggest you be very open with them about what you notice them do or not do with regard to their nonverbal communication. In our home, it's no secret to the Bigs that we read their facial expressions and look for their tells. It actually helps that they know this because it makes them more aware of the messages they're inadvertently sending with their eyes or other gestures. It also helps for them to see examples in their siblings. This is also not an exercise in teaching them to improve their poker face so that they can lie better. They do need to understand, however, that as they move through life, it will benefit them to be aware of the messages they're sending through their nonverbal communications in relationships, be it personal or professional. Just as important, we stress to our kids that they must always tell us the truth—even when they've done something wrong. If they admit their mistakes, we'll work through it together. If they break a rule and then lie to us, all bets are off.

I suggest you be just as open with your kids about what you're observing in their body language and look for opportunities for them to observe it in others, whether it's their siblings or an example of something you know you do subconsciously when you're nervous that you can demonstrate for them. Openly discussing this with your kids helps them to understand how much people can say without any words at all, and when they have concrete examples to observe, that makes it tangible and more understandable for them.

Key Principles to Teach Your Kids About Vetting Information

As you begin looking for ways to teach your children how to examine information they receive from others and read critically for themselves, here's a quick recap of the most important points and some suggestions of practice exercises for you to try with your kids:

1. Establish a relationship of trust with others. Through the use of You Me, Same Same, your child isn't just able to understand another person's perspective; they're able to create a genuine bond. When they form genuine relationships with people, they're creating an environment in which people are more likely to tell them the truth. Moreover, similar to how I was willing to entertain and learn about Ryan's parenting methods because of the relationship we had, your kids may find themselves opening up to other viewpoints they learn from a trusted friend, or they may utilize their persuasion techniques to bring others to their point of view. Encourage your kids to develop close relationships with their friends and emphasize the importance of keeping their word (more on this in chapter 14).

2. Maintain objectivity and an ability to change their minds. It's important that kids have an ability to take in new information and know how to challenge their own viewpoints and hidden assumptions. This can be practiced in a basic and fun way, which also allows your kids to use many of the principles we've already discussed. Have one of your children choose something that's their favorite, something they think is the best—it can be a food (like chocolate cake!), place, movie, book, basketball player, whatever you'd like. For example, they could argue that Michael Jordan was the best basketball player of all time (as someone who spent her childhood in a Chicago suburb in the 1990s, I can vouch that this is the correct and only viewpoint). Then have your other children (or you or your partner if you have an only child) come up with alternatives, such as "No, Steph Curry is the best basketball player," and attempt to change their mind. This is an opportunity for your other children (or you) to practice You Me, Same Same, as well as persuading someone to their way of thinking. It's also an exercise for the first child to take in new information and be open to the possibility of changing his mind. Remember that depending on your child's age, they may want to prove their own point and view this exercise as "winning," so focus on the spirit of the message and not whether they "give in" to the other viewpoints. This is of course a very basic version of the principle we discussed, but you can build on it from here. Once you've done something like this as an illustration, you can then piggyback on it with a discussion on what it means to take in new information and be objective and willing to change your opinion.

3. Practice recognizing mind-sets and biases in the news and other sources. In addition to reading news articles and watching reports to look for examples of bias, you can use social media to teach your kids this skill. I grew up in a home where my parents taught me that two things you never discussed with others were politics and religion, but with the widespread use of social media nowadays, we see people posting articles that share their views on these topics regularly. It may be a good time to examine your own friendships and connections on social media—do most of your friends post articles that have the same views as you? What about viewpoints that are different from your own? See if you can scan through and find multiple different perspectives. Do you have a friend who poses thoughtful questions hoping for a respectful dialogue in the comments? This can be rare, but it does happen. Comb through to find appropriate examples for your kids to see how differently people can look at the same issue. If you can't find any, start a thread on your own profile to generate some thoughtful discussion. Through valuing diversity of thought, your kids will become more aware of their own mind-set and bias as they move throughout life.

4. Learn how to read nonverbal communication. In addition to practicing reading each other's body language within your family, look for opportunities to people-watch with your kids. Sit on a park bench and watch the passersby. What can you learn about people by the way they walk? Do they carry themselves strongly and confidently or are they hunched over and unsure of themselves? When you go out to dinner, find a seat with a wide view of the restaurant. What kind of conversation is the couple across the room having? Is it a happy conversation? Is one of them happy to be there and the other looks disengaged? You get the picture. The more your kids start to look for these visual cues, the more they'll start to actually see.

Whether it's politics, science, diplomacy, or just gossip at school, your kids need to have the ability to judge what kind of information they have, who's given it to them, and how it fits in with everything else they know about the topic. This won't just serve them well as teenagers—this is a vital and important skill that should be exercised and used throughout their entire lives. Kids also need to understand that just like they assess the information others give them, others will judge the information they're sharing. If they want to build and keep relationships with others, it's important that they are trustworthy. They should role-model the behavior they expect from others; for example, tell the truth and be a source on which friends and family can rely. This starts in your relationship with them. The hope is that when the trust is there, your kids will make good choices and tell the truth, and for those times when they don't, they should remember that no one can see through their best poker face like their parents.

CHAPTER TWELVE

NAVIGATING TECHNOLOGY

How to Stay Safe in an Online World

"Hold on, one of the execs is pinging . . . she said she needs to talk right away," Ryan said. "I have to call you back."

"Okay, sure," I said, realizing he had already hung up.

Ten minutes later, he called me back, and I could hear the anxiety in his voice.

"She wants to meet with me in an hour and says it's important. She's never asked me to meet right away like this. Could this be bad news?"

"What could she have to say to you that's bad? I'm sure it's nothing," I said, trying to reassure him, although I couldn't help but feel anxious myself.

Ryan and I both left the CIA in 2015, a year after we married. We considered staying at the Agency when our current tours ended, but we would need to travel overseas or back to Langley, Virginia, and neither of us wanted to uproot the Bigs. They had already changed schools several times as a result of Ryan's previous tours and

subsequent divorce, and our goal was to provide them as much stability as possible. We decided to live in Washington State, where
Ryan grew up, and seek out private sector opportunities there. It was
at this point that I took a position at a Seattle-based tech company,
where I worked as a threat-intelligence program manager in information security and established the company's first insider threat
program to prevent and detect malicious insiders from stealing intellectual property and confidential information. It was also here
that I analyzed advanced persistent threats and malware. I quickly
learned that the biggest threat to my male colleagues wasn't a zero-
day exploit, but instead a savvy, successful woman in a tech role.
Nearly two years after leaving the Agency, I transitioned to a PR role
at the same tech company, and I finally found where all the women
were. I won't say they were hiding, because not only were these
women in plain sight, they were absolute *rock stars*. Ryan and I found
ourselves working together again, albeit tangentially, when he left
his position as a senior security adviser at a national lab and joined
me at the same tech company to lead worldwide security for an in-
novative and confidential business unit.

Ryan had been in his new role for several years on the day he received this phone call from one of his execs. He was successful by
anyone's definition of the word, so I was fairly certain it couldn't be
bad news. But what could be so important for an exec to schedule an
immediate one-on-one meeting with him like this? I waited on pins
and needles to hear how the conversation went until he finally called
me back later that afternoon.

"You'll never believe this," he told me. "It had nothing to do with
work; she wanted advice about her daughter's internet use."

As it turned out, Ryan's boss learned that her daughter had been
communicating with someone online whom she had never met and

had shared personal information with him. Given the exec's high profile and the confidential nature of her position, she was concerned about someone potentially trying to get to her through her daughter. She wanted to know how she could verify that this person was actually a teenage boy like he claimed and whether she needed to be worried. Ryan talked her through it and helped her verify the person's identity through social media targeting analysis, a way of gleaning information about someone through their social media footprint—the same type of open-source research the CIA does before approaching a potential asset. He ultimately called the number his boss provided for the contact via a burner phone and used savvy elicitation to confirm the identity. Then he gave his exec advice for how to talk to her daughter about this issue. He recommended she take her daughter to dinner and have one-on-one time before bringing up the topic with her. He emphasized how important it was to build and maintain a relationship of trust with her daughter because the way she addressed this issue could determine how much her daughter shared with her in the future. (Don't worry—I'll tease out this concept of how to build a relationship of trust with your child in chapter 14.) The exec knew that Ryan's CIA expertise coupled with his parenting experience made him uniquely positioned to answer her questions and determine whether she should be worried about her daughter's internet use.

How Technology Changed the Spy Game

When espionage is depicted in film, it's often full of futuristic technology—freestanding holograms, as analysts swipe through intelligence reports; real-time satellite coverage of intelligence operations; and unrealistic spy gadgets. While there *are* some impressive gadgets and other forms of technology the CIA uses, the reality is that much of the actual espionage that takes place is often done with basic tools and human interaction; that is, *without* the use of technology. Remember when we discussed the importance of knowing how to read a map and find your way around? It's not just because spies should be aware of their physical surroundings for their security. They should also be aware of the technological footprint they're leaving behind. Much of a CIA officer's activities can be traced through their smartphones and various GPS technology, so for this reason and others, they often don't carry their personal phones or use a GPS when traveling to and from an operational meeting.

If CIA officers' activities can be traced via technology, then you can bet your assets' activities can and will be. That means communicating with assets has to be done creatively, which could mean things like dead drops (hiding intelligence somewhere for an asset to pick up at a later time), burner phones, actual covert communications systems that the CIA issues to assets, and other preestablished covert communications and rendezvous points. For example, I once had a planned asset meeting in a third country—meaning a country other than where he or I was posted at the time—that was scheduled for several weeks into my asset's trip to this country, in which he was assisting in its elections preparations. Because he was advising the country's government ahead of its presidential elections, he wasn't entirely sure if he would be able to excuse himself for a weekend getaway at such a busy time without seeming suspicious. I didn't generally meet this asset in this third country, so we didn't have a covert communications system set up. Instead, we agreed to a signal via his public Facebook profile. If he changed his photo to one we had mutually agreed upon within twenty-four hours of our scheduled meeting, it meant that he would no longer be meeting me there, and I'd have to wait until he was back home to debrief him, postelection. It meant the intelligence wouldn't be as relevant or actionable, but it was a scenario we needed to plan for because his safety was more important than timely intelligence.

While the CIA prefers to do much of its espionage in old-school ways largely to avoid detection, the Agency has had to adapt the way it conducts espionage as it has come face-to-face with new capabilities like cameras on every street corner, facial-recognition software, and social media. Things like biometrics can limit the locations an operations officer can travel to for operational meetings, and it can even limit future personal travel.

Other technological advances don't necessarily have workarounds and can't be avoided, which the CIA has learned over time. When social media first emerged, for example, covert CIA employees were prohibited from having personal accounts. However, they found over time that the lack of a social media presence actually drew attention to covert employees—the opposite of what they had intended. As a result, the Agency began allowing personal activity on various social media sites and encouraged a security-conscious approach.

Throughout training, CIA officers are taught to be mindful of what they put online because people can learn a great deal about you from your internet presence. Covert officers were forbidden to connect to overt CIA officers on all social media sites, and in fact, linking to other CIA officers was discouraged even if they shared the same cover or overt status. The idea behind this being that if an adversary found one CIA officer on social media, they could easily find a whole pool of them just by looking through that person's friends list. People rarely followed this guidance, though; after all, when your life is engulfed by the CIA, that's where most of your friends are. Foreign adversaries can also learn what's called targeting information about you—likes, dislikes, hobbies, profession, family life, and more. Just like we look for information when developing You Me, Same Same, like Ryan did in preparation for approaching his target at the local scuba club, our adversaries mine social media and internet sites for similar information about CIA officers and even US businesspeople who have access to corporate intellectual property or any information that would be of interest to a foreign government.

How to Tackle Technology with Your Teens

While your kids likely don't need to worry about foreign intelligence services gleaning information about them through their online presence (unless you're a CIA officer or a certain billionaire who owns the *Washington Post*, in which case you should absolutely worry about this), there *are* unsavory people who are interested in information about children online for nefarious purposes. It's likely that these individuals will look for the same types of information about your kids in order to connect with them, build a relationship, and even to find out their daily schedules and activities. For this reason and others we'll discuss, it's critical to teach your kids to be thoughtful about what they post about themselves online.

Because the Bigs were all under ten when I met them, Ryan hadn't yet established parameters surrounding technology, including the internet and social media use. It wasn't long before these issues started popping up, though—the first being via cell phones—so we got to tackle them together. For our family, we made the decision to get the Bigs cell phones at younger ages than we probably would have if we weren't a two-home family. With them spending some of their time at their bio-mom's house, it was important that we be able to get ahold of them. If this hadn't been the case, we likely would have held off until the kids began participating in afterschool activities and driving themselves. We stress with our kids that the primary purpose of their phones is so that we can get ahold of them, whether it's calling or texting them. Apps are secondary, and they only have access to them once they finish their chores. Additionally, because there are so many apps out there, some of which are questionable as far as appropriate content goes, we don't allow them to add any to their phone without our approval; there is a virtual lock on the phone for downloading new apps until we approve an electronic request from them on our own phones.

We recommend that, at the very least, parents stay apprised of all of the latest apps teens are using, if not exercising some level of control over their access to them. At the same time, it's important to balance these boundaries with independence. We want our kids to have some freedom with their phones so that they can strengthen social skills and stay connected to their friends. We also want to build trust with them through giving them more and more responsibility. That said, we want to set them up for success and not failure, and that's where the boundaries and expectations come into play. In addition to controlling the installation of apps, we also put screen-time limits on their phones, and if they want extra time, they have to ask for it by sending a request from their phones to ours.

Speaking of responsibility, you may find that each of your kids can take on varying degrees of responsibility at different ages. It's important that you examine each app and not only determine what age the app lists as appropriate but also consider your child's level of maturity and responsibility. If they're at an age where you're unsure that they can make appropriate decisions about what to post and what not to post, then that might mean they're not ready for some apps. And you can be sure that at some point, if you haven't heard it already, your kids will say to you, "But, Mooooom . . ." or "But, Daaaaad, *all* of my friends have [insert latest, most popular app name here], and I'm the only one who doesn't have it." They may even follow it up with a real stinger, like, "Don't you trust me?"

That's when you lay it out for them. Of course you trust them, but you also want to set them up for success. Even adults sometimes make poor choices about what to post on social media, and you want to make sure they don't make a decision now that could affect them for the rest of their lives. For example, picture this potential scenario: underage kids are sent text messages with nude photos of other kids in their grade. The kids who receive the texts then forward them, setting themselves up for the possibility of being charged as sex offenders for distribution of child pornography. Yes, it sounds completely absurd that a high school student who receives and then forwards illicit photos could be required to register as a sex offender, but this is not entirely out of the realm of possibility. In fact, many states are grappling with how to handle cases that involve sexting. For example, the Colorado Supreme Court upheld a ruling in mid-2019 to require a juvenile boy to register as a sex offender after he and two girls who were roughly his age exchanged nude selfies.[1] For these reasons, it's important to emphasize to your kids that one impetuous bad decision has the ability to follow you on your record for the rest of your life.

Some parents opt to install some type of surveillance software, like Life360 or mSpy.[2] We've chosen not to do this for the Bigs because we feel that the boundaries we've put in place along with the other CIA concepts we've taught them about getting off the X, security awareness, and how to think critically work for us without the help of software like this. That doesn't mean there aren't times when I'm anxious about what could happen to them out in the world. When these thoughts creep up, I remind myself that while there's a lot that's outside our control, by teaching our kids how to be security-conscious and think critically, I can feel more confident in their ability to think on their feet and stay safe. Every situation is different, and every family has its own relationship dynamics, so it's important that you choose what's best for your own situation. I do recommend, however, that if you choose to install one of these applications, you discuss it openly with your children. Nothing erodes trust faster than your child finding out that you were spying on them without their knowledge.

In our home, we try to find a balance between giving our kids access to various apps that we feel are appropriate and saying no when we feel for whatever reason they're not ready. Again, it's about balancing boundaries and independence. We're particularly mindful of being at one extreme or the other. For instance, we have several friends who don't allow their teenagers to have any social media apps. That's right—zero. While I understand the logic behind this because it *can* be a slippery slope, Ryan and I want to give our kids the opportunity to learn and make mistakes while they're with us and can seek our guidance, and they can't do that if their access is restricted entirely. At the other end of the spectrum, we know parents who allow anything and everything when it comes to cell phones, apps, and technology. This, as you can imagine, can create situations in which your kids may make the wrong choice, either intentionally or unintentionally. What we've found works for us is to consider each app for each child on a case-by-case basis. We've made it clear to the Bigs that if we've told them they can't have a particular app, that doesn't mean we're not open to changing our minds with the right persuasive argument and data points. However, an argument that hinges on "But this app is so *in* right now!" or "*Everyone* has it but me" will not get them anywhere. Instead, we ask them to answer the following questions (this structure should look familiar to you from chapter 9):

1. What do you want?
2. Why do you want it?
3. How will you use it?
4. What impact will it have on your daily life?
5. How do you envision this changing your life in the short and long term?
6. What opportunities will having this app give you?

If they can answer these questions respectfully and convincingly, then they've just argued their way into an additional app. If instead they're complaining or being rude, then nothing will change, and we won't approve access. Just like choosing what level of supervision you'll have on their cell phones is different for each family, this will be a personal choice for your family. Find an approach that works for you and your family; ideally, it's one that emphasizes trust so that if and when your child makes a mistake using technology, they feel comfortable enough to seek your guidance. We'll discuss more about trust and your kids in chapter 14.

-RYAN-

WHEN SAFETY LEADS TO SAVVY

Another reason why Christina and I prefer to be in the middle of the spectrum in terms of what we allow our kids to have access to when it comes to technology is because it's important to us that they're technologically savvy, while also being safe. If we restrict our kids' access too much, we're taking away opportunities for them to become more skilled and knowledgeable. For example, I once had an asset who was a foreign diplomat serving in a senior leadership position overseas. Together with a specialist I flew out from Headquarters, I met the asset in a third country so that we could train him on our covert communications (COVCOM) system, or the clandestine way we would communicate to share information and plan future clandestine meetings. Following the asset's return to his foreign posting, he had trouble using the COVCOM on which we had carefully trained him. This meant I had to meet him again in another country and fly out yet another specialist to train him a second time. This took up time and resources, not to mention the additional operational risk it created. Not everyone has the resources or access to be tech savvy, but it's increasingly becoming the "language" we need to survive and thrive in the twenty-first century. Because we're fortunate to live in a situation in which our children have access to the latest technology both at home and at school, we want to make sure they know how to use it. So instead of shying away from technology out of fear of what our kids may be exposed to or mistakes they may make, let's help them learn how to safely use it in a way that helps them to be savvy and successful throughout their lives.

Toddlers and Technology

While you'll have the ability to equip your teens with many of the CIA-based skills we discuss, it will of course take some time to teach these concepts to your toddlers and younger kids. You may not have the stress or worry about managing their social media use just yet, but that doesn't mean technology won't come into play in your day-to-day life with young ones. In fact, there are some fantastic ways that technology can enhance and support your life as a parent of toddlers. For example, I've mentioned my postpartum anxiety and alluded to a few of the tools that helped me. When Ari was an infant, I relied on a special Bluetooth-enabled sock so that I could monitor his heart rate and oxygen levels from my phone. When he became a toddler, I purchased a GPS tracker for him to wear under his clothes anytime we left the house. It may sound extreme, but it was right after Gigi was born, and I was awash in anxiety just at the thought of managing them both at the park. Ari wasn't yet two years old, and I was terrified that I would lose sight of him and someone would take him. For that situation, I chose to take advantage of technology for his safety and, quite frankly, my peace of mind.

I've heard some people say that these types of devices prey on anxious parents, and I'd say that's not entirely untrue; however, I found them to be immensely helpful in giving me the peace of mind I needed. That said, there is such a thing as too much of a good thing. If you choose to use one of these or other similar monitoring devices, even basic baby monitors, try not to become obsessive about it. Make sure they're set to alert you when necessary, and set boundaries for yourself on when you'll check it manually.

Of course, with all good things comes the potential for bad, so with that, let's talk tablets. First, we'll start with the good, because there is so much good with these. They offer educational games for our toddlers, and they can also be a welcome break for parents trying to cook dinner or simply sit down for thirty minutes of solace without anyone touching or pulling on them. We strive to monitor screen time for the Littles in the same way that we do for the Bigs. Kids love routine, so I try to have set periods of time when they can expect to watch shows, and it's usually because I have something I need to do. I let them know that they'll watch one (sometimes more!) show, and that when it's over, I'm turning it off. It helps them to know before the show starts that it's the only or the last one and prevents a situation in which they ask for one more at the end. Sometimes they still do, but it helps when I can remind them that I already told them this was the last one.

That's not to say we don't have days when rules go out the window and they watch much more than usual for no apparent reason other than I just don't have it in me to "mom" anymore that day. And sometimes, life throws you giant curveballs. For example, during the COVID-19 pandemic the lines between home, school, and work blurred, and many families—ours included—relied on screen time more than I care to admit. But when we're not trying to stay sane during quarantine, we strive to have as much of a structure surrounding this as possible. As for using an actual tablet rather than a TV, I've found that when my kids have control over a tablet, it makes it that much more difficult to take away, so I save the tablet for times when I'm really desperate, like if I need to bring them along to my doctor's appointment or on an airplane. Otherwise, it's put away because "it's charging." (It's a good thing toddlers don't realize how long it takes batteries to charge, because that excuse wouldn't work for me anymore!)

Key Principles to Teach Your Kids About Using Tech Safely

Whether you have young kids and are still formulating your approach to technology use or you have teenagers and are looking for ways to make adjustments, here are some tips that Ryan and I both believe are important to emphasize with your kids:

1. Don't overshare personal information online, especially with people you don't know. I can't stress enough how important it is to teach your kids this principle in order to keep themselves and your family safe on the internet. When I was growing up, chat rooms had just started to take off. I made a few new friends in one related to a punk rock band I liked, and we even met up in person at a concert months later. I wouldn't dream of doing this now or allowing my kids to do it! The reality is that with the accessibility nowadays—that is, more and more people online and more and more apps for our kids to use—the possibility for your kids to encounter someone with ill intentions has become increasingly likely. Talk to your kids about what it means to be catfished, in which a person uses photos of someone else online to disguise their true identity. They should understand that if they haven't talked to someone in real time, like in a video chat, they can't confirm that person is who they say they are. Your kids should also understand that even if they do talk to someone in real time, it doesn't mean they really know the person. They still shouldn't give details about their personal life and daily activities, and they should be mindful of photos they share online, keeping all settings on private/friends only.

2. Be aware of how predators can use information about you. In addition to talking to your kids about You Me, Same Same to help them build rapport with others, help them understand that someone could use this same approach with them for nefarious purposes. Whether it's an intelligence officer, criminal, or sexual predator, this person will look for as much information about someone as they can find to help them develop a successful approach. If your kids encounter someone online who seems to know a lot about them or with whom they have an awful lot in common, they should consider that it may not be a coincidence. Online predators are savvy, and they'll look for your child's interests, activities, and maybe even information about when and where your child will be somewhere. When you discuss these topics with them, it's a good time to review their security awareness skills as well. In short, you should have a goal to be aware of whom your kids are talking to and what they're sharing, while allowing them as much independence and privacy as possible. It's a balancing act, and the levels of comfort and independence will vary with each family.

3. Guard your future. One of the lessons we stress repeatedly with our kids is the permanence of what they post online and how it has the ability to impact their future—in a positive or a negative way. Research from CareerBuilder indicates that 70 percent of employers review a candidate's social media activity, and more than half of those employers have chosen not to hire a candidate based on what they've found online.[3] I recently had a conversation with a young relative about this, in which I was as direct as possible. He was in his early twenties and had made a habit of posting his drug and alcohol use on his very public Instagram page. I told him that he might feel proud of these decisions now and think that he'll always feel this way, but the reality is that we change so much throughout our lives. Thirty-year-old you will not be the same as twenty-one-year-old you. I told him to do his future self a favor and at least make his account private. That doesn't mean the risk is completely gone, but it does decrease it by giving you *some* control over who sees the information. However, you should emphasize to your kids that once you've posted something online or sent it to a friend, you've lost control of that information. You have no idea whose hands it could end up in—regardless of whether your account is private.

I'm not saying that your kids shouldn't have a social media presence or that they should be afraid to post anything at all. Just like the CIA realized that letting their employees have some social media presence was better than none at all, your kids' social media presence, when done appropriately and responsibly, could actually help them get a job in the future. In fact, 43 percent of employers said that they hired someone because of something positive they saw on their social media accounts that either confirmed the person's expertise or demonstrated the candidate was well rounded.[4]

3. Protect yourself from cyberbullying, and stand up for others. When talking about technology use, a topic that comes up more and more frequently today is cyberbullying. Kids, and even adults, sadly, have found that it's easier to say horrific things from behind a computer screen than in person. In fact, most people wouldn't dream of saying to someone's face the types of things they say online. The National Center for Education Statistics conducted a survey in 2017 that found 15 percent of students in grades nine through twelve said they had experienced bullying in the previous twelve months. Of those in the 15 percent, 27 percent reported that the bullying had somewhat or a lot of negative effect on how they felt about themselves, 19 percent said it negatively affected their schoolwork and relationships with family and friends, and 14 percent said it negatively impacted their physical health.[5] One of the Bigs shared with us that she's very careful about posting anything political online because she's seen what has happened to some of her classmates. For example, when one young woman posted a photo wearing campaign paraphernalia for a political candidate, she received more than a thousand negative comments and even death threats. When the school principal was made aware of the death threats, rumor has it he said that she "brought it on herself." Our Big noted, and I tend to agree, that the classmate's post seemed like it was meant to gain attention and stir the pot, given the context in which she was wearing the attire. However, that certainly didn't mean she should have received death threats in response to the photo. It also doesn't mean that anyone should have to censor their own political beliefs for fear of others, a lesson we want to be sure our kids understand. At the same time, it's a fine balance between teaching our kids not to be afraid to share their views on the world and showing them how to use discretion and maturity in what and how they post. Some of these skills will come only with age and life experience, but we hope that with your guidance, your kids can avoid missteps.

More than anything, when it comes to cyberbullying, we want our kids to understand the importance of being kind, whether it's in their interactions with others online or when they see someone else experiencing bullying. For example, Hunter's friend, the one who I mentioned was wrongfully accused of sending offensive texts, experienced cyberbullying during that period. Not only was it important that Hunter find out what really happened straight from the source, but we also used it as a lesson for him to show kindness to someone who really needed it. After a conversation with him about this, he asked us to take him to the store so he could pick up some ice cream and some of his friend's favorite candy to drop by her house. Her dad met him at the door, thanked him for being such a good friend to her, and said how much it meant to him and her mom that he came by during such a difficult time for their daughter. It's little things like this that can make a difference for someone.

Technology can be tricky, but it can also be fantastic. Our kids are growing up with so much information at their fingertips, so instead of being scared of the ways it could negatively impact them, let's help them use it to their advantage. Through prepping our kids and teaching them to be security savvy when it comes to technology, we're giving them the tools they need to set themselves up for a successful childhood and ultimately a successful adulthood.

CHAPTER THIRTEEN

TAKE OWNERSHIP

How to Gain (and Earn) Responsibility

"Are you sure they need an allowance?" I asked Ryan after we were first married. Supporting three children who lived in two households felt like enough of an expense for a brand-new marriage—did we really need to give them their *own* money too? After all, I never had an allowance growing up. I viewed it as a privilege, and an unnecessary one at that.

"Yes, they need it. It's so they can learn financial principles and responsibility," Ryan told me. I finally understood what he meant when I saw these principles in action on a trip to the mall with the Bigs as we were preparing for our first Christmas together as an official family.

"Okay, you guys have an hour to do whatever Christmas shopping you want," Ryan said as he handed out each of the kids' debit cards and reminded them of their available balance. He had set up checking accounts linked to debit cards for them as early as the bank would allow so that he could start teaching them. Ryan had a rule with the Bigs, though, and he stressed it over and over. They were only to use their debit cards to withdraw money from the ATM—they were not for making purchases. This was a hard-and-fast rule that the kids knew and respected. However, Ryan wanted to use this Christmas outing as a teaching example. He told the kids, "Hey, we don't have much time. Just use your debit cards to make purchases . . . no need to withdraw cash from the ATM." The kids didn't blink twice, and away they went.

Ryan stood either in or outside each store and watched as the kids excitedly bought Christmas gifts for each other and other family members. He knew exactly how much each of them had in their accounts, and he was prepared to stop them if they were about to overdraw. He watched as they continued to make purchases, blissfully unaware of the speed at which the balances in their checking accounts were dropping. At the end of the hour, they regrouped.

"How much do you guys have left in your accounts?" he asked them.

"I think I have about forty-five dollars," Hannah said.

"Yeah, I probably have around forty," said Hunter.

"Twenty-five," Lena said confidently.

"Not exactly," Ryan began. "Hannah, you have fifteen dollars left. Hunter, you have eleven seventy-five, and, Lena, you have five."

Their jaws dropped to the floor. Ryan went on to explain to them how easy it can be to make purchases using a plastic card—so easy, in fact, that you can lose track of how much you've spent rather quickly. This wasn't the first time Ryan had shared this point with the kids, but it wasn't until this illustration that it really hit home. Sure, they each blew some money in the process—and I got some really cute Christmas ornaments from them that year—but they'll never forget this lesson.

With Great Power Comes Great Responsibility

The CIA gives its officers an overwhelming amount of responsibility, ranging from financial independence to analytic opportunities. As an analyst, I was responsible for my own financial accounting for my temporary-duty assignments, which often meant accounting for thousands of dollars due to most of my travel being to Africa. Later, when I began my field assignment with the DO, I was given a revolving fund of several thousand dollars each month from which I could pull to wine and dine assets and pay in exchange for foreign intelligence. Our meetings were one-on-one, with no other witnesses to vouch that I had actually paid my asset the amount that I claimed I did. I'd come back with a "receipt," which was essentially a handwritten index card that I had created myself and had the asset sign. Not quite as high-tech as the movies make the CIA look, right?

It wasn't just financial responsibility that officers had at the CIA. Less than a week into my new top secret career, the Ethiopians invaded Somalia in an effort to overturn the Council of Islamic Courts (CIC) and stop it from expanding its influence across the central and southern parts of the country. Although I was a brand-new analyst, I found myself writing about this invasion in the President's Daily Brief. I quickly learned one of the greatest parts about working at the Agency: they trusted you with a great deal of responsibility from day one.

While I was writing analyses for the president, Ryan was running clandestine operations in the field, where, for example, he was entrusted to run surveillance-detection routes on his way to meet his assets. He and his asset were to arrive at the meeting location at the exact time—they couldn't be late, or even early. They had to arrive within a two-minute window. It was his responsibility to arrive at his clandestine meeting without anyone following him. If he didn't know he was being followed and mistakenly brought surveillance with him to the meeting, he put his asset's life in danger. Many assets who choose to work with the CIA are doing so at great risk to their own lives and their families' lives.

When the CIA entrusts its officers with huge responsibilities like keeping their assets safe so early on, it knows it isn't trusting just anyone with these responsibilities. Each person who walks over the Agency seal on the floor and past the stars on the wall at CIA Headquarters has gone through extensive background investigations and psychological testing. And before we ever gained regular access to classified information, we were thoroughly trained for a range of scenarios. It was in these training scenarios that we could fail, but in real life, there wasn't much room, if at all, for that.

-RYAN-

SECRETS AND SIRENS

I experienced this responsibility and independence at the CIA right off the bat, during my first tour overseas, fresh from the Farm. I was entrusted to take over handling a senior-level foreign government official who always had a wealth of intelligence to share. Because this asset was one of the Station's most prolific reporters, he needed to be handled and debriefed carefully each meeting, and of course protected, as the security of the asset was paramount. Although I was still a green operations officer, I was entrusted to run the source and continue moving the case forward; there was no room for error. The chief had mentioned on several occasions the importance of this asset, and I knew there was a lot at stake if something were to go wrong.

I was walking through the old part of the city one evening after another successful operational meeting with this asset. I felt confident and secure in my tradecraft as I clandestinely carried my bag of intelligence. This was my favorite part of the city, not just because of the picturesque cobblestone streets, but because the changes in elevation and twists and turns made it the perfect surveillance-detection route. I was about halfway through my route back to the office when I heard sirens. At first they were coming from only one direction and so distant that I could barely make them out. But they kept getting louder and louder, and soon, I could hear them coming from multiple directions. I wasn't nervous—I knew no one was following me—but I began to wonder what was going on.

I turned down a long street and had walked about a hundred yards when I saw the first police car with flashing lights coming right toward me. I looked to the side street to my left and saw a police car barreling down that road too. I then glanced behind me and saw another car coming from the rear. Now I was nervous, but true to my training, I remained calm. It appeared as if all the police cars were convening on the exact location I was standing. Well, let's be honest, it wasn't "as if"—they were! And I had a brief-case full of secrets! Had I been followed? No way, I thought to myself. How had they found me? I followed my training; I had done everything by the book. So what had gone wrong? I continued walking while the police cars converged. Should I run? But what would that accomplish? Even if I got away, they knew who I was and would just meet me at my house. I did the only thing I could do: I kept walking and played it cool, thankfully. I say *thankfully* because if I had started running, they likely would have started to chase me. Instead, I watched as they exited their vehicles and ran into the building adjacent to me. I kept walking. While I walked, I smiled, because little did they know they had just run past a spy with juicy intelligence under his arm.

How to Introduce Responsibility to Your Kids

So how do you prepare your children for this type of independence and responsibility when we live in a world where helicopter parenting is rampant from the moment the child is born? When you give your kids independence and responsibility from a young age instead of doing things for them or hovering over them, they're learning and gaining skills that prepare them for adulthood. Just like the CIA prepares its officers for the real world of espionage by training them for the extremely large amount of responsibility they'll have, we want to prepare our kids to make smart, responsible decisions throughout their lives. Whether these decisions are financial or otherwise, the best way to do this is to teach them early and provide a safe space for them to make mistakes. And you can't do that without giving them some responsibility, so start small and build from there.

"Okay, Ari, close your eyes," Ryan said as Ari scrunched his eyes and held out his tiny, three-year-old hands. Closing his eyes for surprises had become one of his favorite things to do, so much so that he regularly asked multiple times throughout the day if he should close his eyes for even the mundane things I'd give him, like his lunch.

"Here it is!" Ryan said as he placed the small leather pouch he had personally sewn for Ari into his hands.

"What is it?" Ari asked excitedly.

"It's your very own money pouch," Ryan explained.

What Ari was experiencing was another rite of passage for Hillsberg children. Each of the Bigs had received their own money pouch at about three years old; that's when Ryan started introducing them to coins and allowing them to make their own purchases. I didn't come into the picture until the Bigs were older and already handling larger denominations of bills and coins and regularly making their own purchases. It was eye-opening for me to now be involved with the process from the start.

It became Ari's responsibility to carry his money pouch and know where it was at all times. The fact that it contained only a modest amount of coins helped ease any anxiety I had about him losing it, and at the same time, it built Ari's confidence. From there, we began to give him the freedom to occasionally make his own purchases when we were at the store, discussing with him "wants" versus "needs" and what he could afford based on the amount of coins in his money pouch. (This doubles as regular lessons in counting money for toddlers, which is an added bonus!) I now knew that someday, this would evolve to look like it did with the Bigs, who did things like walk over to the local eatery with friends to purchase an after-school snack, buy their own movie tickets, and pay for snacks at the football concession stand on a Friday night. And with Hannah, it included more sophisticated tasks, like making insurance co-payments at the doctor's office and paying and tipping her hairstylist.

Key Principles to Teach Your Kids About Independence

The idea of financial responsibility and independence in our home includes extensive conversations with the Bigs about loans and interest. According to Northwestern Mutual's 2018 Planning and Progress Study, the average millennial (age eighteen to thirty-four) had about $36,000 in debt, and one in five expected to die without ever paying it off.[1] Just because this is common doesn't mean these statistics have to include your kids. Ryan began these conversations with the Bigs as soon as he felt they were old enough to grasp the principles. One way you can do this is by having conversations with them about what not to do—a cautionary tale—using examples from people they actually know or fictitious people you've created to illustrate the point. For example, you can discuss with them the importance of building good credit so that they can do things like rent an apartment, activate a cell phone, or take out a mortgage. At the same time, you can share with them an example of someone who used her credit card to pay for things she couldn't afford and how her credit card bill increased each month as the interest continued to compound, making it more and more unlikely that she would ever be able to pay it off.

1. Give kids plenty of hands-on experience with money. The best way for kids to learn these principles is through their own direct practice. After all, we'd much rather they learn through making mistakes when they're young and with us than after they've moved out of the house and are managing their own finances. For example, when the Bigs were younger and wanted to buy something at the store they couldn't afford, Ryan would offer to give them a loan. Before they'd get too excited, he'd remind them that they'd have to pay him back with interest.

"Wait—why would I owe you $13?" Hunter would ask.

"Because of interest," Ryan would tell them.

"What's interest again?"

"When you're borrowing money that isn't yours, it isn't free. It comes at a cost. Whoever you're borrowing from, whether it's a bank or a person, adds on a percentage over the amount of time it takes you to pay them back. So you end up paying more than what you would have if you had enough money to buy the item outright without a loan," he explained.

"Well, that's not fair."

"Maybe not, but that's how interest works, guys."

"Then why do people do it?"

"Well, think about it . . . people don't necessarily have enough cash on hand for larger purchases like vehicles and houses, so auto loans and mortgages give them the ability to purchase them and pay it back over time. When all is said and done, they end up paying much more than the initial cost of the item."

2. Introduce the concept of loans and credit in age-appropriate ways. From there, Ryan would usually discuss how credit cards are another way to borrow money and explain how they come with their own risks because it can be easy for those types of purchases to get out of hand. It's important to talk to your kids about only buying things that you have enough money to purchase and teach them that the purpose of a credit card is to build credit. Period. Full stop. It is not to buy things that we can't afford until we get paid next week or next month. We use them for things like filling our gas tank, and then we immediately go home and pay off the card with money that we have in our checking account. This is necessary so that you build credit, which is required to qualify for a loan.

Loans, particularly student loans, can be a fantastic option—Ryan and I both used them to pay for our college educations. However, we want our kids to understand what they're taking on when they sign on the dotted line, because I know I didn't. I had a job on my college campus at the Speech Production Laboratory, but I did it more out of personal and academic interest than a desire for money, as it didn't pay much. I remember having a rude awakening when I started paying back my loans after I began working at the CIA. I had taken advantage of the six-month grace period after graduating to start my payments, naively thinking there were no strings attached. I had no idea that during those six months, I was accumulating even more interest. Had I understood the concept of interest and just how much money I was taking out, I may have chosen differently. Maybe I would have spent more time working my way through college so that I could make payments all along, like some of my friends did. Or maybe I wouldn't change a thing. Thankfully, I was able to pay back my loans with my new CIA salary. Things could have gone differently for me, though—and simply put, it's best to go into something with eyes wide open. So while these may seem like basic conversations, the fact is, many parents don't have them with their kids, evidenced in part by the alarming debt statistics I mentioned.

3. Look for chances for your kids to practice independence outside your home. In addition to preparing your kids for financial responsibility, you should give them opportunities to act independently. In order to do this, you have to get *out of the house!* Taking your kids out frequently is crucial in building important life skills like independence and responsibility. It can be so easy as a stay-at-home mom to stay indoors with your kids, especially when you live somewhere like the Pacific Northwest, where it rains much of the year, like we do. I've aimed to get out of the house with the Littles at least one day a week since they were infants so that they can interact with people and, when they're able, learn to speak for themselves. I'll be honest, in the beginning, this was more so that *I* could interact with people and not go completely insane alone in a home with a newborn and later a newborn and a toddler.

When it was just Ari and me, we went out for lunch multiple times a week along with other outings to parks, zoos, aquariums, and museums. Outings don't always have to cost money though. One week we may go to a local museum, and the next week we'll visit a new park and bring packed lunches along. When Gigi arrived, we continued life as usual as best we could, but it became trickier, of course. However, it was important to me to have kids who knew how to behave in restaurants, and I believed (and still do) that the only way they can learn this skill is if they're given the opportunity to actually eat at restaurants. For us, that means we don't use phones or tablets to entertain our kids at the table. Instead, they can color or play with a few small toys, like plastic dinosaurs I keep in my bag specifically for times like this, but absolutely no screens. I know screen use at the dinner table has become more and more common, so if this is you or has been you in the past, please do not feel judged here. We've all had those moments when we just need to survive, and screens give us our best chance. I fully confess to using them at home when I need to get things done or when I simply feel like taking a mental break from parenting. But if you can, I implore you to resist doing this at restaurants as best you can. I consider the tablet like opening a can of worms—once it's introduced in a setting, toddlers then start to expect it. And like I mentioned previously, there's something about kids having a tablet in their hands and feeling like they have control over it. Once you've set a precedent of allowing tablets at restaurants, it can be difficult to rein in.

My recommendations don't have anything to do with arbitrary boundaries or the amount of screen time doctors and other experts recommend for children. What it comes down to for me (and Ryan agrees) is that when we allow our kids, whether toddlers or teens, to disengage from the table at a restaurant and enter their own world on their screen, we're missing out on an opportunity to engage with them and teach them important life skills, like how to behave at a restaurant, how to order their own food, and simply put, basic table manners. Likewise, we don't allow the Bigs to have their phones out at the table, whether we're at a restaurant or at home. When your kids become old enough to participate in dinner conversations, take advantage of that time to connect with them.

When you're out, look for ways for your kids to exercise independence. For example, I look for opportunities for Ari and Gigi to go up to the counter to talk to the cashier alone, like if we need to ask for extra napkins, silverware, or a to-go box. You can look for similar opportunities for your kids. It can be something as simple as asking someone where the restroom is or ordering their own food off the menu when you're out at a restaurant—with supervision, of course. We learned this the hard way when Hunter ordered himself a filet mignon at our wedding rehearsal dinner, instead of ordering from the kids' menu! When the server arrived and asked who ordered the filet, we all sat there befuddled, until eight-year-old Hunter raised his hand from the other end of the table and nonchalantly said, "Oh, that's mine!" We couldn't be angry with him for ordering the most expensive item on the menu because we were so proud of him for engaging with the server and ordering himself a meal—and a classy one at that! (If anything, it was the server who likely should have checked with the parents before putting in his order!) During these outings, have your kids bring their money pouches along to make those purchases we discussed, and eventually, this will evolve to include things like making trips into the store by themselves to buy a few items, or maybe something that sounds a little less scary to you, like letting them ride their bikes around the track at the park while you look on from a bench nearby.

This can look different the older your kids are. For example, if you have teenagers like we do, you may start dropping them off at the movie theater or mall alone, or you can allow them to do a solo outing to your local town or city. We often let the Bigs have "Seattle days," where the three of them can explore the city without a parent for the afternoon or the entire day. It helps that there are three of them—we don't recommend sending only one child into a large city alone. If you have only one child, consider allowing them to do this with a trusted friend, so long as the friend's parents are on the same page with this level of independence. Make sure your kids have a map (that they've ideally studied beforehand) and a cell phone to call you in case of emergency. Establish a meeting time, and then set them free to explore the city through shopping, eating, visiting museums, or whatever they choose. At the end of the day when you regroup, talk to them about how they spent their day. Find out what they gravitated toward and what skills they found useful. Was there anything they were afraid or uncomfortable doing? Knowing this will help you learn what you can spend more time on with them, and perhaps you do the next trip into the city or town together to help build their confidence. This type of solo outing for your kids is particularly important and useful because it combines many of the skills I've recommended you teach them; it's a chance for them to exercise financial responsibility, independence, security awareness, navigation, and, if necessary, getting off the X.

Of course, all these outings became very different, and even temporarily nonexistent, during the COVID-19 pandemic when we all had to stay close to home. In fact, there were many months in early 2020 in which we could leave our homes only for necessities, making it next to impossible to find opportunities for our kids to connect with others in person and to practice responsibility and independence. Experiencing a pandemic forced us to be creative and learn that sometimes we may have to look for virtual options to help our kids learn these skills. In our family, we leaned heavily on phone calls, video chats, and some virtual story times we found online. NASA's story time from space has become one of our favorites— what kid doesn't want a story read to them by an astronaut? When communities slowly started opening up again, each family was faced with a decision on how to interact with others in a new environment filled with masks and new terms like *social distancing*. It's important to realize that circumstances can change and as parents, we need to adapt and look for alternative solutions for our kids.

4. Know your child. It's also important to keep in mind as you're dishing out more responsibility to your kids and helping them to learn independence that each child is different. We strive to have the same expectations and standards for all our children, but we recognize that some of our kids thrive on more structure and need more rules than our other kids. And while some may gravitate toward rules, they may also need to loosen up a bit. In short, what may be an appropriate level of responsibility for one may not be for another.

For example, I could already tell how different Ari and Gigi were even as toddlers. When Gigi was born, I could set up an activity for Ari while I put her down for nap, and he would quietly occupy himself for as long as I needed. Keep in mind he was only twenty months old at the time. Nearly two years later, when Gigi hit this age, it occurred to me how unusual it had been for Ari to do that, because Gigi, like many twenty-month-olds, was very busy and wouldn't sit quietly for an activity for even a few minutes, let alone the amount of time Ari had when Gigi was a newborn. Ari is naturally very rules-oriented, much like Hannah, which means it can sometimes be easier to give him more responsibility because we know he'll follow the rules since it's in his nature to do so. At the same time, he can view the world in a very black-and-white way, so having a dad like Ryan, who views the world in shades of gray, is very useful for a child like Ari. Gigi, on the other hand, is a spirited child who needs to have very clear boundaries and structure before she's entrusted with responsibility.

You may have already observed some of these differences in your children. The key is meeting them where they are and realizing your kids may not have the same level of responsibility at the same ages. It may vary; some may earn more responsibility at a younger age, or they may have to wait longer before being allowed to do certain activities on their own. Strive to find balance between keeping it fair and age-appropriate for each child's abilities.

If some of this responsibility and independence sounds like a little too much for your parenting style, find what feels comfortable to you. Don't be surprised if when you start to exercise some of these techniques you experience judgment from others. For example, I was with Ari and Gigi at the park one morning when they were two years old and one year old, when a man drove into the parking lot from the main road and got out of his car to yell at me and a girlfriend of mine who was there with her twins, who were Ari's age.

"Don't you think she's a little young to be over there by herself?" he asked in a judgmental tone.

We looked over at Nicole's daughter on the play structure about thirty feet away from us, and exchanged confused glances.

"Well, I'm right over here changing her brother's diaper, and I can see her just fine," my friend replied.

That's when we realized he was referring to a little girl on a bike on the other side of the track, who he assumed was one of ours.

"Oh, her? She's not our daughter. I think that's her mom walking on the track," I said as I pointed to the other side of the track.

The man looked disgusted, huffed and puffed, and walked back to his car. He had actually spotted a child on her bike and pulled over to chastise her parent, who he believed was too far away to be parenting properly.

What is an appropriate distance, though? And what's an appropriate amount of independence and responsibility? That's just it— everyone's idea of what's appropriate will vary. It helps to remember that these are skills that you can build up over time. When I began to see this topic as a progression of responsibility and independence, almost like building blocks, I finally started to understand why Ryan felt comfortable parenting the Bigs with a longer leash than initially felt comfortable to me. The idea of dropping my kids off curbside at the grocery store had been completely out of the realm of possibility for me, and if I'm perfectly honest, it still gives me some anxiety (and probably always will!). But here's the thing—none of this is done in a vacuum. The Bigs haven't just learned about responsibility and independence; they've learned it together with the other concepts we've discussed, like how to get off the X and how to be aware of your surroundings. These skills all work in concert with one another to help your kids become confident, security-conscious, and resilient.

CHAPTER FOURTEEN

PROTECT YOUR ASSETS

How to Keep a Promise and Live Your Principles

"I'll probably have the Talk with him sometime this weekend," Ryan said as we were driving into town for a dinner date. Hunter's eighth birthday was coming up, and Ryan had planned a bowling alley party with close friends and family. I wouldn't be there, of course, since I hadn't met the kids yet.

"The Talk?" I asked. Did he mean a sex talk?

"You know, the Spy Talk," he said nonchalantly.

"No, I don't know. What do you mean 'the Spy Talk'?"

"Oh, I thought I mentioned it. When the kids turn eight years old, I tell them I'm a spy," he said, as if it was perfectly normal to share such an enormous secret with a child.

"You do?! What if they tell someone?" I asked worriedly.

"They won't," he said confidently. "I did the same thing with Hannah when she turned eight."

His confidence wasn't enough to convince me that telling kids that their parent was a *real-life spy* was a good idea. It seemed trusting them with important, potentially life-threatening information such as this was never a good idea. Ryan, however, felt differently. And while I questioned his judgment, I knew he was someone who, at the end of the day, valued loyalty and trust beyond all else. I also knew that there was no one more important to him than his kids. So what gives?

The Importance of Trust

In a spy's game, and Ryan's job specifically, one of the most important things to do is protect your sources. This can be done only with loyalty, trust, and the ability to keep your word. No one is going to betray their country with someone they can't trust. It's an operations officer's responsibility to protect everything from the source's identity when they write up the intelligence they receive from them to their physical safety while meeting with them.

Remember how I said I didn't want to date, let alone marry an operations officer because so many of them were smarmy? Many of them believed that in order to do their work they needed to do smarmy things, like drink lots of booze on the job and go to scuzzy places like strip joints with their assets. One of the reasons it was so refreshing to meet Ryan was because he showed me that you didn't have to do that to succeed. And, in fact, you could actually be a *more* successful operations officer if you *didn't* do those things.

Think about it—you're a foreign government official considering cooperating with the United States by sharing classified information about your homeland, which means you'd be committing espionage, a crime punishable by many years in prison in some countries (if you're lucky) and death in other countries (if you're not so lucky). Don't you want to know that the CIA officer with whom you're meeting and sharing this sensitive information is protecting your identity, and by extension, your family's as well? In this hypothetical example, would you rather meet with the CIA officer who gets sloppy drunk with you at the Da Club or the CIA officer who isn't under the influence and is always in control? Whom do you trust more?

I wish it went without saying that even if CIA officers met my definition of smarmy, something they never, under absolutely no circumstances did was blackmail someone for intelligence. Our foreign enemies may use those tactics, and Hollywood may love to portray espionage in that way, but in the case of the CIA, it's categorically false. Much of this relates to reputation. The CIA wants to be known as an intelligence service that people want to work for—other countries' intelligence services don't necessarily have that reputation. If you're considering committing espionage, wouldn't you choose the service that takes the best care of you? (This begs the question why anyone in their right mind would defect to Russia—ahem, Edward Snowden—but I digress.)

These values weren't just demonstrated by upstanding operations officers like Ryan and a select few I had the honor of working alongside (that's not to say that there aren't many more I didn't encounter!); they underpin the very foundation of the CIA.

"We're the good guys," a man said in my training class as I was preparing for my field assignment in the DO.

"Do you think Russia takes care of its assets after they get all of the intelligence they need from them? Hell no, they don't. But we do. No matter what it takes," he said. He went on to tell several stories of the lengths the CIA goes to in order to protect retired or compromised assets and ensure they're appropriately compensated for their efforts. Indeed, there are countless accounts of assets the CIA has taken care of over the years. For example, sometimes an asset is in such a sensitive role that it's not safe for them to receive payment while they're active operatives for the CIA; large amounts of money could raise red flags and draw attention to them. In these cases, the CIA keeps the money in special accounts for them to receive later or whenever they need. If the asset passes away, the Agency tracks down the person's family and ensures the money gets to their next of kin. In many of these cases, the family has no idea their relative cooperated with the CIA.

-RYAN-

WHEN THE CIA GOES THE EXTRA MILE

I experienced how much the CIA genuinely cares for its assets first-hand when I orchestrated the retirement party of all retirement parties for a CIA asset I was handling. He had been on the books for more than thirty years and was an extremely seasoned asset, knowing more about clandestine operations than the many green operations officers he came in contact with over the years, including me. Unlike most clandestine meetings, the situation in which I met this asset was unique in that we met in his home due to serious health issues he was facing at the time. In so doing, I developed a strong relationship with the asset as well as his wife and adult children. In fact, it wasn't unusual for me to join them for a family dinner following our debriefings, and to this day, I haven't found food as delicious as his wife's cooking. To be honest, he was one of my favorite assets in all my years at the CIA. When it came time for this asset to retire, I worked diligently to find as many of his previous handling officers as possible and invited them to Headquarters for a special ceremony for him and his family. Together, we thanked him for his years of service and rewarded him with a handsome bonus as a way to thank him. Of course, not all assets are given such pomp and circumstance—so you can imagine how useful and impactful the intelligence must have been—but all assets are shown loyalty and protection because, as Christina's instructor said, we are the good guys.

Creating a relationship of trust and loyalty with CIA assets was one thing—which Ryan happened to be quite good at—but how could you possibly expect so much from an eight-year-old? I mean, I understood sharing your spy secret with your partner. In fact, the CIA actually recommends that you *do* tell your spouse what you do for a living, rather than your cover story. This hasn't always been the case. Indeed, in the past, operations officers often kept their classified jobs a secret, but they found that this could actually hurt rather than help marriages. Moreover, the CIA knew that when a spouse was up to speed on the job, they could become more useful in operational situations where the CIA officer needed to wine and dine a target with his or her partner. But what was Ryan's logic for looping the kids in at such a young age?

It all came down to his ultimate goal of creating that relationship of loyalty and trust with them, and he believed in starting it from the time they were young. And when they reached eight years old, he knew that they understood the concept of keeping promises and that he could trust them not to tell anyone his secret. But how exactly did he do this? And what made him so confident?

For starters, Ryan decided that he would use the phrase "I promise" sparingly with the kids. It can be so common to hear those words tossed around, and he knew he didn't want to do that. He wanted to ensure that the kids knew that when Daddy said, "I promise," he always followed through on his word, and each time he did, it furthered that foundation of trust he was building with them. Cementing this principle early on can eliminate stress for kids because they know that when Mom and Dad say, "I promise," they mean it. I've seen the look of relief on the Bigs' faces when they're asking for something and then they hear those two magical words. It takes away any concern or question for them because they know that when Ryan says them, it's a done deal.

If I'm honest, I don't think I truly understood what this concept meant to Ryan until years into our marriage. The words "I promise" somehow didn't carry as much weight with me. I'd throw them around the way we did in middle school when we put out our pinkies for a pinky promise.

Perhaps this is why when Ryan told me before we married that he had to get a Rhodesian ridgeback at some point because he "promised the kids one," I didn't think much of it.

Oh, they're just kids, I thought to myself. *Just nod and say yes. The kids won't care what kind of dog they get, as long as it's a dog. You can convince him to get a doodle later.* Again, I didn't realize what "I promise" meant to Ryan and what it already meant to the Bigs.

I think these words can be especially powerful when you're a single parent, as Ryan was when we met, and perhaps some of you reading this may be as well. He wanted to be certain that the Bigs understood that although the promise he and their bio-mom had made when they married didn't last, it didn't mean other promises he made as their father wouldn't. One of those promises was that they could all live with him (and later that became us) as soon as their bio-mom would allow it. We discussed this one before we married too, and I told Ryan that of course I'd support the kids living with us. I knew how important it was to him.

At the time, it seemed years away, if it was going to happen at all.

You can imagine my surprise when weeks after we married, Hunter got the green light to come live with us full-time. Now, here's the tricky part—Ryan and I had just bought a home together, but he was working several days a week in another part of the state. That meant that as a twenty-nine-year-old newlywed, I was caring for my ten-year-old stepson for multiple days and nights at a time until Ryan returned home.

Truth be told, I wasn't ready for this. I had moments when I wished more than anything that Ryan would take back his word. How was I supposed to care for my new stepson all by myself? I didn't know how to cook for myself, let alone a child too. I was thrown into full-time stepmotherhood without much notice, but now, as a more seasoned stepmom and mother, I understand that sometimes that's how life goes. It doesn't always happen on our schedule. Case in point, two years later, just after Ari was born, Hannah and Lena moved in with us full-time too. Ryan felt like he finally had all the pieces of his heart in one place, and we were able to grow together as a family. Sometimes that growing involved growing *pains* as I adjusted to life with a newborn and three older kids while at the same time learning the ropes as a new working mom. All that growth, though, the good and the sometimes painful, was entirely possible because Ryan kept his word to the kids, and I kept my word to him.

Trust Is the Key with Our Kids

Similar to how loyalty and trust is a two-way street between a CIA officer and his asset, one of the greatest parts about instilling this type of loyalty and trust with your kids is that it goes both ways. We trust our kids with information, and because we've built that foundation, they also trust us. In the same way that we protected our assets' identities, we protect our kids. What I mean is that the Bigs know they can tell us anything, and so long as there aren't legal obligations with what they've told us, we will do everything in our power to protect their identity. Once they have this assurance, they're more willing to open up because they know that they can trust us in the same way that we trust them. For example, one of the Bigs recently told us a story about a party that went awry when the kid's parents came home and discovered their daughter had hosted a party in their absence. Our Big, whom we'll simply call Big in this story (I'm purposely being vague here to protect the source), told us how thankful they were that they'd chosen not to go to the party, saying they'd had a bad feeling about it. (They didn't actually know that it was an unsupervised party when they were invited and decided not to go.) During that conversation, we coincidentally learned that a friend of mine's daughter had been at the party. A few nights later when I met my friend for dinner, conversation landed on the party, and I asked what her daughter had told her about it.

"Oh, she wasn't there. We didn't let her go, thankfully," she said. Then, after a pause, "Why are you asking? Did Big tell you she was there?" she asked, becoming increasingly flustered. It was clear to me that her gut was telling her that her daughter might have not been truthful with her.

"Oh, no—I must be confused. I swear they said she was there, but I think I got my lines crossed," I said. I immediately started worrying that I'd said something I shouldn't have. Had I really gotten mixed up and misheard the evening before or did Big tell us this information in confidence? Either way, I needed to be sure. I excused myself to the restroom, where I called Ryan.

"Was Kylie at the party on Saturday night or am I confused?" I asked him.

"She was, but Big forgot to tell us that Kylie didn't tell her parents she was there. There's some sort of cover-up going on," he told me.

"Well, shit. I just told her mom. I didn't realize it was a secret," I said.

"Whatever you do, make sure Kylie doesn't find out it was Big who told us. Big will never trust us again."

Shit. Shit. How would I fix this? I couldn't lie to my friend and say I was mistaken when I knew the truth. She knew me too well anyway; she'd see it all over my face as soon as I returned to the table. Her daughter had been lying to her for several days, insisting she hadn't been at that party. If the roles were reversed, I'd want her to tell me. So I said this:

"I'm sorry, Angie. I hate that I have to be the one to tell you this, but Kylie was at the party."

"I knew it!" she said, and immediately reached for her phone.

"Wait! Please don't call or do anything now. If she knows you're at dinner with me, she'll immediately know it was Big who ratted her out, and it wasn't purposeful. It was just that Big was telling us about what happened. They feel terrible that they screwed up their friend's cover story. And if you blow this, then they'll never tell us anything again either. We'll all lose access—for both of us."

Wow, I had really made a mess of this. I'd had no choice but to come clean with Angie about her daughter's whereabouts because

(1) I had already put my foot in my mouth, and (2) if she knew something about my kid, I'd expect her not to leave me in the dark. The least I could do was provide her the same courtesy. But how could I keep her from calling or running home immediately and making this situation even worse?

"Please give it till morning," I pleaded with her.

She sighed. "All right, but it's going to kill me sitting on this information!"

When I got home, I immediately had a talk with Big. I couldn't take a chance that this would blow back on them and for them to think I had betrayed their confidence. I explained that I hadn't realized it was a secret and how I had put my foot in my mouth but then recovered and resolved the situation.

"It's okay—I didn't tell you it was a secret. I understand," Big said.

"Don't worry. She's not going to say it was you," I said.

This situation was tricky for several reasons. Even if I hadn't put my foot in my mouth initially when I didn't know that the information was a secret, wouldn't I still have needed to find a way to tell Angie somehow? Like I said, if she had this information, I'd want her to tell me. Let me be clear about something, though—I'm not talking about contacting *any* child's parent to make sure they know what their kids are up to. Angie is one of my closest friends, and we look out for each other. If this were someone whose parents I didn't know or perhaps knew to a much lesser degree, I would consider it none of my business and wouldn't dream of sharing the information. In this situation, however, even if I had known that there was a cover-up, I still would have told Angie. However, I would have come up with some way to share the information with her while also protecting my source, Big. I could have done a better job at this and not made my faux pas if I had known all the information up front.

In these types of situations, there will never be a clear, black-and-white, right-or-wrong answer for how to handle them. However, I recommend you approach each one with an eye toward protecting your source—your own child—before you decide how to handle the information. This way, you're prioritizing your relationship of trust with them above all else.

Key Principles to Teach Your Kids About Trust and Loyalty

One of the best ways to teach your kids how to keep promises is to actually live these principles yourself. Here are some of my quick tips for teaching your kids loyalty and trust:

1. Use the phrase "I promise" as sparingly as possible. By limiting the times you use this phrase, you're sending the message to your kids that these are not throwaway words. They carry weight and should be treated as such. If there's ever any pushback or concern as to whether you'll do something your kids are asking of you, this phrase offers the peace they need, but only when you've given it the appropriate weight it deserves.

2. Keep your word. When you do choose to say, "I promise," always follow through, no matter what. This helps your kids to learn that when you use those words, it's a sure thing. You can't forge long-lasting, trusting relationships with your partner or your children without keeping your word. If something happens that is out of your control and it affects your ability to keep your promise, communicate that with your child so that they understand. Life happens sometimes, and we're only human, which means we can forget things. Be sure to distinguish between falling short because you didn't take the promise seriously and falling short because you're human and had too much on your mind. You should do everything in your power not to forget or break a promise. Set an alarm on your phone, write it on a sticky note or on your hand, do whatever you need to do.

3. Know how to say I'm sorry—to you partner and to your kids. This one is so important in building a relationship of trust. When you make a mistake—and for parents it's *when*, not *if*—say you're sorry. When Ryan and I have a disagreement or get into an argument in front of the kids, we make it a point to apologize to each other in front of them, even if we've already resolved it behind the scenes. We want our kids to see that reconciliation. Likewise, if we've done something to our kids that warrants an apology, we swallow our pride and say, "I'm sorry." This one has been especially humbling for me as a stepmom, particularly all those times I lost my cool thanks to pregnancy hormones. Trust me when I say that there's nothing more humbling than apologizing to your teenage stepchildren for something that seemed totally rational at the time yet you later know was batshit crazy.

4. Use your own discretion when determining what and how much to share with your kids. There are ways to emphasize loyalty and trust that don't necessarily include sharing secrets or private information that may not be appropriate for little ears. Use your best judgment when it comes to the types of information you choose to share with your children. Each family is different. For example, it wasn't until I became an adult that my mom started sharing with me whom she voted for in previous presidential elections. Perhaps it was a generational thing, or maybe it was just what she thought was appropriate or not appropriate to share with kids, but when I was growing up, she always said religion and politics were off-limits. In your family, you and your partner can decide what is or isn't off-limits with your children.

If you're lucky enough that your child is already sharing private information with you, congrats! You've built a trusting relationship with them. At this point, you need to do everything you can so as not to jeopardize the progress you've made, by protecting the source. If you're not quite there yet, just know that each time they confide in you, or you in them, you're taking baby steps toward that trusting relationship. And each time you keep your word when you've promised them something, that's another stepping-stone on your way there. In order to truly arrive at this relationship, you need to protect your source along the way. This will require some living in the gray, as you'll have to balance this need with any ethical obligations you feel in telling others the information you learn. Of course, if there are legal obligations or ramifications of such information, then that's a different ball game. In those situations, I recommend being as honest and open with your child as you can, so that they understand why you need to share the information, but you should still do everything you can to protect your source.

I recommend you begin incorporating this important principle of keeping promises with your children through open and honest communication as early as possible so that it becomes naturally ingrained and part of the way they view the world. This will help your kids in their own lives as they build genuine relationships with others—whether it's colleagues, friends, or romantic partners.

CHAPTER FIFTEEN

PERFECTION IS THE ENEMY OF THE GOOD

How to Mitigate Risk (and Still Live Your Life)

I was the perfect stepmom—before I became one myself. I had all these ideas of how I'd parent the Bigs once Ryan and I married. I wanted so badly to do it right. Of course, I wanted them to like me, but most of all, I wanted to prove to myself, to them, and to everyone else who thought I was certifiably insane for marrying a divorcé with three kids that not only could I do "the stepmom thing," I could do it *perfectly*.

In the beginning, I followed Ryan's lead when it came to parenting the Bigs. But not just on the CIA concepts I've discussed throughout this book. On absolutely everything. We wanted to be sure that the Bigs accepted me as their stepmom, so we were very careful about who did the disciplining and how. I was also careful to keep my cool, even when it was the last thing I wanted to do, because I was hyperaware that my relationship with them was teetering on new ground. It would be a while before we felt a sure foundation under our feet.

I would sometimes feel the weight of this pressure and break down in tears.

"I can't be perfect." I'd say to Ryan. "I'm not always going to do the right thing or say the right thing to the kids. I need some grace to mess up."

"I never said you had to be perfect," he would always say.

"No, but if I ever lose my cool in even the slightest, you're quick to give me a look or my phone vibrates with a text from you from across the room telling me what I should or shouldn't have done," I'd say.

He didn't deny that he did these things, and he continued to insist that no one expected perfection from me, but I went on trying to achieve it just the same.

That all went to shit when I became pregnant with Ari and my hormones went wild. I was no longer able to keep my temper in check at all times. I wasn't as measured in everything I said and did. I experienced what I call hormonal rage. It wasn't necessarily directed at the Bigs, but sometimes it was. I can't say with certainty what happened because I've blocked it out to the best of my ability, but some of the highlights—or lowlights, as the case may be— include when I threatened to "tuck and roll" out of the car because I was so displeased with the outfit Ryan was wearing to a barbecue (the kids weren't there for this one, thankfully, and I wasn't actually serious—at least, I don't think I was. But seriously, who wears a wool sweater with a dirty ball cap and flip-flops to a barbecue?), shattered a glass in the kitchen, and threw a sippy cup across the floor (this was in the early postpartum days). Who was this monster? I certainly didn't recognize her.

Getting Comfortable with Imperfection

As the youngest of three kids myself, I mastered the art of reaching perfection at an early age. Where my older brother and sister fell short, I picked up the slack. My parents never had to tell me to do my homework or even review it for me. In fact, I managed to create an internal pressure to achieve—and achieve perfectly at that—all on my own. You can imagine my disappointment when I received my one and only A- my junior year of high school, which meant I would be *salutatorian* of my graduating class instead of valedictorian, like I had envisioned for myself for so many years. I cried in my room for days and struggled with giving myself the grace and mercy I so desperately needed.

It's not a stretch to consider how someone like this could end up at the CIA, particularly as an analyst. When I began in the DI, I found myself surrounded by people who were a lot like me. We were the competitive overachievers, the nerds, the know-it-alls, the experts. And here we were in one place, working together to keep America safe and advise our nation's president.

Being an analyst can be a lot more black-and-white than being an operations officer. Analyzing such large swaths of data takes someone who is meticulous and thorough. Writing intelligence assessments requires not just expertise but an ability to write clearly and concisely—dare I say perfectly. More than anything, policymakers want to know that the analysis they're reading is accurate. When it's not, you can bet your ass you're going to hear about it. And when it's a big enough mistake, you'll even hear about it on the news as an "intelligence failure." Mind you—for every notable intelligence failure, there are many more intelligence successes, although you won't hear about those. The running joke among CIA analysts is that there are only intelligence failures and policy successes.

Perhaps these perfectionist tendencies were accentuated the most during CIA analytic training, when most analysts were brand-new and wanting to do everything just right. Because I had started at the CIA as a foreign media analyst, I was already a year and a half into my career when I transitioned to the DI. The influx of new analysts at that time meant I had several months on my new team before there was space in the Career Analyst Program (CAP), the intensive analytic training that all analysts were required to take. It was early 2008; I was covering sub-Saharan Africa, and we were writing about it regularly for the president. By the time I went to training, I was confident in my ability to write intelligence assessments and therefore had a bit more perspective than some of my newer colleagues.

Several weeks into CAP, we were completing one of the most intense and stressful weeks of the training program, an intelligence task force. Here's how it worked: Instructors created a realistic scenario, like a terrorist attack. You were given bits of fictitious intelligence over the course of several days, and you and your team developed an analytic assessment of the situation, including who was responsible, impact to the United States, and opportunities for US engagement. (These should sound familiar to you from our writing tutorial in chapter 9.) You produced individual and team papers for the president and other US policymakers and conducted individual and team briefings for instructors role-playing important US leaders. You often worked late into the night to keep up with the amount of information the instructors threw at you.

I went into the training having heard of several analysts who mentally and emotionally broke down during the exercises due to stress brought on by tough instructors and ruthless editing. I knew I didn't want that to be me. The confidence I had in my ability to write and brief prior to this training allowed me to take a step back and see it for what it was. Yes, they wanted your intelligence assessments and briefings to be perfect. We were the cream of the crop, they kept telling us, but at the same time, I knew I needed to find a balance or I wouldn't survive. Everything came into focus the evening we did the "uncertainty and ambiguity exercise."

"All right, I'm done for the night," I said as I closed my computer and prepared to head to my room, just down the hall. We were staying at an undisclosed CIA training facility with overnight rooms complete with 1980s furnishings and wallpaper—to call it a hotel would be a stretch. It was already nearing 9:00 p.m., and with my work done for the night, there was nothing left to do but sleep until doing it all over again in the morning.

"You're done?" Ken, the analyst sitting across from me, said with shock and disbelief in his voice.

"Well, yeah . . . it's an exercise in uncertainty and ambiguity. No matter how long I stay and look at the intelligence, I'm not going to find a 'right' answer," I said.

Ken didn't know what to say. He, like many other analysts, was certain that if he stayed long enough and pored over the data, he'd find the correct answer. What he and those other perfection-seeking analysts were missing was the fact that there *was* no correct answer. The exercise was about learning to deal with uncertainty, because in intelligence analysis—and frankly, in many things in life—you're going to encounter situations in which you don't have enough data or you have conflicting data. It's your job to appropriately weigh this data and caveat it in such a way that you're accurately representing both the information and your confidence level in your analytic assessment for US policymakers.

I found this perspective equally important when I went through operational training in preparation for my DO field assignment years later. Unlike in DI training, where they tell you that you're the cream of the crop and expect perfection, the DO takes a different approach. They break you down by putting you through training that is designed for people to fail, because when you fail, you learn from it, and you'll never make that mistake again. As I've mentioned, the DO wants everything you experience in training to be a hundred times harder than real life so that whatever you encounter in the real world will be that much easier for you when you're operating in the field. This too requires a healthy dose of perspective so that you're not seeking perfection.

-RYAN-

THE GUINEA PIG

I had been at the Farm several months, and things were getting more real for us in training. We were learning new concepts that were helping us think on our feet. It was on one such day that I was chosen to be the guinea pig for a role-playing exercise, in which I was going up against one of the instructors, who was pretending to be an asset. This was a hotel meeting, and I was supposed to debrief him for intelligence. My classmates and the remainder of the instructor team were watching and listening through a glass wall. As we exchanged pleasantries, my instructor, "the asset," started writing something on a piece of paper and slid it across the table. The paper read: SHHHH . . . THEY'RE LISTENING. THEY CAN HEAR US.

For some reason, I thought this was a lesson in how to talk my way out of a dangerous situation. Somehow, the asset knew the room was bugged. I wanted to make sure that I didn't say anything to compromise him or myself, so I continued to have a casual conversation with him, in hopes of not discussing anything that may be alerting to the fictitious foreign intelligence service that was eavesdropping on us. Again, the instructor wrote on the paper and slid it across the table. This time, it read: I'M SCARED. WHAT DO WE DO?

I continued to casually talk with the asset, essentially ignoring his written messages, partly because I was frazzled and also because my primary concern was to ensure that our conversation flowed naturally without awkward pauses. After a few more minutes of conversation, the instructor stopped the exercise and broke out of character. He informed me that I had failed—miserably.

I soon learned that what I should have done was take the piece of paper and write back questions for the asset to answer, all while continuing the conversation. I should have written questions like, WHO'S LISTENING? HOW DO YOU KNOW THEY'RE LISTENING? I should have also guided him and given him instructions on how to get out of the scenario. In hindsight, it was obvious to me what I should have done, but when you're frazzled and in the heat of the moment, sometimes you can't see it. Even though I knew this was an exercise that was designed to make me fail, I was so focused on winning and performing perfectly that I wasn't able to think logically and quickly on my feet. What I thought was the perfect response to the situation blinded me to the logical, commonsense response that I should have had to the asset's written pleas. Everyone in the room learned a valuable lesson that day because of my failure, and it was in this way that the instructors guaranteed that none of us would ever make this same mistake in real life.

The pressure in DO training is just as intense as in the DI, and arguably more at times, since you know that at least one person is going to fail each exercise, and you don't want that person to be you. It can be easy, especially if you're prone to perfectionist tendencies, to be blinded like Ryan was in his exercise, or to do things like stay in the office late into the night doing your paperwork "just right," instead of getting the rest you need ahead of your next training exercise in the morning. What you'll find, however, which Ryan and I both saw in our training, is that the people who stay late into the night writing up their meetings in the required operational cables are often too tired to successfully complete their training exercises the following day. They find themselves making silly mistakes because they're simply not as alert as they need to be in order to do things like execute a successful surveillance-detection route, for example.

The principle of "perfection is the enemy of the good" is particularly important for an operations officer when handling an asset who is a prolific intelligence reporter. If you spend too much time writing the many (and yes, there are many) supporting operational cables for the case as well as the intelligence reports, you'll quickly find yourself overwhelmed. It won't be long before that one case is taking away from the rest of your caseload and your ability to recruit more assets. Like Ryan mentioned, he sometimes leveraged analysts because they can be force multipliers in a case—not to mention they can share some of the workload. For operations officers, it's impossible to be subject-matter experts on everything, so if they can have an expert come to the debriefing with them and help write up the intelligence reports, why wouldn't they? That way, they can focus on writing the operational cables and move on to their other cases. I used to think this made operations officers lazy, but now I realize it's actually quite smart. Officers in the DO have to see the forest for the trees and learn how to prioritize their cases and time, and understanding when "good is good enough" helps them do this. This same principle can be valuable for you as parents and for your kids.

Parenthood Is the Cure for Perfectionism

I wasn't just the perfect stepmom pre-stepchildren; I was also the perfect mom before I had a baby. I had all these preconceived notions about what I would and wouldn't do. I'd sleep-train as early as possible. My babies would sleep in their own bed. I'd never nurse in public; my baby would be on a feeding schedule so I could always do that in private. And I'd never dare bring my baby to a restaurant; those are for adults trying to get *away* from kids.

Of course, all this went to hell too as soon as Ari was born. None of it was a surprise to Ryan, who had already been through the newborn stage three times. Perhaps it was all to be expected. As with anything, people often think they know something or understand it until they're actually in that situation themselves. What I definitely didn't expect—and Ryan couldn't prepare me for—however, was the pressure I would feel to be the Perfect Mom, courtesy of social media. Where else can you see such a put-together mom with perfectly put-together children in coordinating outfits (but not *too* coordinating because that would be too obvious, right?)? The Perfect Mom manages to set up activities for her kids, who are always well groomed, successfully run her own business, and have dinner on the table by 5:00 p.m., without a hair out of place. And the Perfect Mom? She never loses her cool in a hormonal rage.

During those early days with Ari, when I was up all hours of the night nursing him, I'd scroll. And scroll. And scroll. The more Instagram posts I saw, the more anxious and lost I'd become. Who was I now that I was a mom? Exhausted. Overwhelmed. Anxious. Far from perfect. Certainly not a perfect mom. Or a perfect stepmom. That's when I began searching and found the women who openly talked about the struggles new moms go through. I started to feel like I had gained entrance into an elite sisterhood that I didn't realize existed among women: motherhood. But even in these posts that humorously shared common mom struggles, the content looked carefully curated.

This was highlighted even further during the COVID-19 pandemic in 2020, when everyone was home. It seemed every mom felt the need to post on social media each and every "perfect" activity they'd set up for their kids, or their daily routine for said kids. Texts began rolling in from several of my mom friends:

MOM A: What activities do you guys have planned for your kids today? I'm running out of ideas.

MOM B: I'm setting up a sensory bin with animals.

MOM C: We're trying this new painting activity I found on Instagram. Here's the link.

MOM A: Those are too messy. What else you got?

ME: Umm, I'm going to let my kids ride their bikes and play outside while I sit and watch from the Adirondack chair.

MOM B: Hmm . . . what about freezing toys in ice and having them dig them out like archaeologists?

MOM A: Oh good idea. I'll try that.

Wait, should I have answered differently? Why wasn't I thinking up fun activities for my kids? I noticed all my working mom friends, who were now working from home, killing it in the kids' activity department. Perhaps it was because they were desperately trying to busy their kids while they conducted conference calls, but I couldn't help but think, *Is this what people think stay-at-home moms do all day, every day? Or worse, do other stay-at-home moms actually do these activities every day? Have I been falling short and didn't even know it?* Sure, I did activities for and with the kids, especially on the many rainy Seattle days we have all winter long. And before quarantine, we had occasional outings to museums and zoos during the week. But why did I now feel like I needed to step up my game?

Instead of falling back into my old perfectionist ways, I've had to learn how to take a step back from this content and reach for that perspective I learned at the CIA. When we're deep in parenting, like, really in it, we can believe with our whole being that we need to be perfect, that we need to keep up with all the other perfect-looking moms we see on social media. But the reality is that our kids don't need us to be perfect. They need us to be real. They need us to teach them when good is good enough. I want my kids to have the perspective that I didn't have when I cried for days over that A- years ago. So whether that means shutting off or moderating your use of social media or throwing out that daily routine you felt pressured to make, find what you need to do to gain that perspective and balance.

It was also during this time period that the Bigs were participating in online learning because of COVID-19, and one night I found myself scrolling through posts on a Facebook group for our school district's parents. There was one post that particularly caught my eye. The mom was explaining how overwhelmed her freshman daughter was with the new school format and that she was often spending nine to ten hours a day on her school assignments. She wanted to know if others' kids were having the same experience. I scrolled down through the comments; each one read similarly: "My daughter is spending the same amount of time! This is crazy!" It wasn't until I scrolled through about twenty comments that I finally found one that said, "This hasn't been my son's experience at all. In fact, I feel like most days he doesn't have nearly enough work to do." I sighed with relief. That sounded more similar to what I had observed with Hunter's experience thus far as a freshman at the same school. Nonetheless, I panicked a bit, thinking perhaps he wasn't putting in enough effort. He had been finishing his work for the entire week in just a handful of hours on Monday after the week's assignments were posted. Should we be worried about his grades this quarter? I immediately approached him about it.

"Hunter, are you taking easier classes than some of these other students? I read these comments that some kids are spending ten hours a day, every day on their schoolwork right now."

"Aw, nah," he said, waving his hand, not at all concerned. "Those are just the kids who overthink everything."

"Okay, and you're sure you're getting everything done and you're doing your best?"

"Yep," he said.

And that was the perfect (pun intended) example that told me that Hunter understood what we've been trying to teach and model for him all along.

🍼

"No, you can't have the mac and cheese because you already had pizza," I told Hannah.

"Well, but you said we could split it," she protested.

"But then you opted for the pizza, so Lena gets the mac and cheese," I said.

"I didn't opt for pizza. You said that there wouldn't be a lot, and we'd need to eat something else too," she continued to protest.

"Listen. You opted for pizza the moment that pizza hit your mouth. It's over. I don't want to hear any more. The mac and cheese is Lena's."

"But . . . but . . . Christina . . . wait."

"That's the end of it!"

Whoa. It seemed as though my hormonal monster was making a reappearance. I hadn't seen her in a while, but here she was again in full force.

Hannah and Lena were arguing over who got the leftover mac and cheese from the pot I'd made for Ari and Gigi. We tried not to make mac and cheese often in our house—mostly because we want our kids to eat the kinds of food we eat ourselves, which does not include mac and cheese—but I like to keep a few boxes on hand for the Littles for when I'm in a pinch. It was always a competition between the Bigs on who could claim the leftovers first. When there was enough, I would sometimes let them split the spoils. For whatever reason, I couldn't handle the vultures swooping in for their macaroni on this particular day, and I let loose.

"*That's it!*" I yelled. "*Next time, no one gets their leftovers. I'll either save them for them to eat the next day or I'll throw them away!*" It was an out-of-body experience. I could see myself yelling, all the while thinking, *What's your problem? It's mac and cheese.* I looked over at Ryan, afraid of the disapproving look I might get. I turned around to start doing the dishes. Scrubbing the pan was surely a safe way to work out any remaining rage, right?

I waited for the inevitable vibration of my phone with a text from Ryan about how I needed to knock it off. *It's just food,* he'd say. Instead, I felt him come up behind me, put his arms around me, and kiss me on the cheek.

"I'm sorry," I said. "I'm just tired of them fighting over mac and cheese, and I'm tired of her countering me. When I say no, it means no."

"I totally agree," he said. Moments later, I headed to Hannah's room to apologize. I knew it had been a miscommunication, and I also knew I had overreacted. Before knocking on the door, I stopped myself. I could hear Ryan softly talking to her inside her room, explaining that she needed to be respectful when we say no. I heard her continue to counter even him, and I felt grateful. Grateful to have a husband who had my back and gave me the grace I needed to unleash my frustration—to be imperfect—and grateful to know that my stepdaughter was treating him the same way that she had just been treating me. Somehow, that meant I had made it as a stepmom. What more could I want than for them to feel comfortable enough to challenge me as any teenager would their parent—be it a bio- or stepparent?

Key Principles to Teach Your Kids About Perfection

Just like we can't be perfect, our kids can't be either. Set them up for success, knowing that they'll sometimes fail. And when they do, be there to teach them and help them learn from their mistakes. In fact, they'll learn the most by making mistakes. More than that, help them learn to recognize when good is good enough. Here are some tips to keep in mind:

1. Teach them to work smarter, not harder. In order to do this, you must prioritize your time and not be afraid to accept help from others. Just like Ryan utilized analysts to help him with his prolific intelligence reporter, learn how you can utilize other resources and make better use of your time. When you're so focused on making one specific task perfect, you could be dropping the ball on other things, or perhaps worse, working yourself to the point of exhaustion. For example, when Ari was first born, I found it difficult to lean on anyone else to help me, and as a result, I found myself well past the point of exhaustion. It wasn't that Ryan and the Bigs didn't offer to help; it was just that I didn't accept their offers. I wanted everything done *perfectly*, and only I could accomplish that, of course.

Over the past several years, I have learned to happily accept #ALLTHEHELP, whether it's letting the Bigs watch the Littles when I need to write or exercise or asking the Bigs to unload the dishwasher, among other chores. This means I've had to let go of my expectations for how things should be done (side note: How do they *still* not know where to put the ramekins?). No, they aren't done exactly how I would do them, but they're done. When we start to let go of our idea of perfection, it's amazing all the things we can accomplish. (Full disclosure: this remains a daily struggle for me.)

2. Show them what failure and determination look like. I'm sure it won't come as a surprise to you that from a young age, I've avoided things that I might fail. (Perhaps the valedictorian story gave it away?) I don't know if it was learned behavior or if it was simply in my DNA; I tend to think it's the latter because I've already witnessed some of the same tendencies in Ari, beginning at only two years old. I'm sure it started rather naturally, but at some point, I began avoiding new things if I thought I might not be good at them—or worse, that I'd fail miserably. In as early as first grade, I would feign a headache so that I could spend PE class in the nurse's office and avoid whatever sport we were doing that day, even kickball. It's only been since becoming a parent that I've made a significant effort to change this about myself. Why? Because I do not want my kids to fear failure.

I think of all the things I haven't tried over the years, specifically how I've robbed myself of opportunities to learn new hobbies and sports. And who knows? Maybe I would have been good at some of them, maybe not, but the world is not black-and-white. We don't have to be rock stars or failures. We can fall somewhere in between, and in the best-case scenario, we walk away well rounded and better because of it.

In my effort to discover new interests after becoming a mother—my very own "scuba diving" so to speak—I decided I wanted to learn how to wakesurf behind our boat. I tried to surf nearly every time we went on the boat that summer, often for an hour at a time. The Bigs, who were all naturals and able to surf almost immediately, watched me fall again and again, wondering just how much longer they'd have to sit through this painful display. But I kept swimming back to the board and calling out, "Ready!" as Ryan revved the engine for another go. Each time, I told myself that I was doing this to show the kids that (1) it's okay not to be good at something, (2) you're never too old to try something new, and (3) when we fall in life (or quite literally, in this case), we get back up and try again. I'm proud to say that after an entire summer of determination, I made substantial gains in my wakesurfing abilities. I may not be able to let go of the rope for more than thirty seconds yet, but I'm happy and proud of how far I've come. And that's enough for me—for now.

What's your wakesurfing? How can you model failure and determination for your kids? Is there something new you can try either together or separately? Show them what it means to push through something that doesn't come naturally to you or to them. Encourage them to try something that's new to them or perhaps doesn't play to their strengths. You may not realize it now, but demonstrating lessons like this—and giving them opportunities to do the same—while they're young can have a big impact on how they approach new hobbies and interests throughout their lives.

3. Help them recognize when good is good enough. It took me a while to get on board with this concept, if I'm honest, probably because I've long operated on more of a "Be the best" sort of motto. Let me clarify, though, that when we say good is good enough, it does not mean that Ryan and I don't expect greatness from our kids. Because we do. In fact, our Hillsberg annual theme that we chose for our family in 2019 was Total Domination—in school, sports, work, and life. What we *do* mean when we say good is good enough is to teach your kids how to have a healthy, balanced approach like the one that Hunter demonstrated during online learning. For example, if you notice your child putting more hours into their schoolwork than you know others are, talk to them to try to understand why. Do they need extra help on certain subjects or is this a time-management issue? This is not an excuse for your kids to slack off either. No, they don't have to be perfect, but they do need to try their best. Help them learn to identify and know what their best is and when they've reached that point. It's a fine balance, and it's one they'll need your help to learn.

Remember that this concept that perfection is the enemy of the good starts with you. When you model a more balanced approach, rather than a perfection-seeking one, you're showing your kids that they can do this too. And the less they fear failure, the more confidence they'll have to try new things and add to their repertoire of skills and knowledge. Just think of all the material they'll have for You Me, Same Same!

CONCLUSION

"I don't want to wear that shirt, Mommy. I want this one!" exclaimed Ari as he pulled a striped button-down shirt out of his closet.

"Are you sure you want to wear that? And with your shorts? It's going to be hot today," I told him.

"Yes, I want to wear this! It's my spy shirt."

"Oh?" I asked.

"Yesirree!" he said proudly.

I had no idea what made that shirt his "spy shirt," other than the fact that it resembled the button-downs Ryan sometimes wore to work, so I figured that must be it. I decided to let this one go. After all, if he overheated, he could always take it off and wear his undershirt. How could I turn down a spy shirt, anyway?

❧

Ryan and I made the decision not to wait until Ari and Gigi turned eight years old to tell them we were once spies. We've talked about it openly since Ari was a baby. After all, we're writing a book about it, so it's hardly a secret anymore. I know that at only four and two years old, they don't understand what being a spy really means, but I also know that they will someday.

The Bigs, on the other hand, are all in high school and preparing for college, having had plenty of years to absorb the fact that we were once spies and that we've done our best to instill our CIA techniques in them. When I met Ryan, he wasn't looking to get married again or for someone to help him parent his kids. In fact, he prided himself on being a very engaged dad; he was confident he had his parenting style all figured out. Yes, he was making sure his kids were security-conscious and well rounded, but he was most focused on creating opportunities for adventure. It only made sense that he would lean on his operational experience at the CIA to do this. Ryan's admitted on more than one occasion that he had never considered what a CIA analyst's perspective could bring to the equation. Over the past several years, he has learned what it means to parent with an equal partner who has a CIA background of her own, and sometimes that means compromising and reining himself in.

For me, getting on board with Ryan's CIA-inspired parenting approach meant that I could parent from a place of strength and peace, rather than anxiety, uncertainty, and a desire for perfection. More than that, I could lean on my own CIA training and experience and leverage it in a way I had never considered. We may approach problems and tasks differently at times, due to our varying CIA backgrounds and personalities, but we're a team. The fact that you're reading this book right now is a testament to that. The reality is that we're still learning, and each day brings new challenges and ways that we can continue to teach our children using these CIA principles.

My hope for you is that you'll use these same techniques I've shared with you to shape your kids into security-conscious, confident, and well-rounded children. At the same time, I hope that I've also given you peace of mind and eased at least some of your anxiety. Your kids won't do everything right 100 percent of the time—hell, neither will we—and they won't remember all these principles. That's why repetition and understanding are key. And while we can't take away all risk for them or expect them to avoid all risk themselves, we *can* mitigate the realistic risks. We can provide them the skills they need to be safe and prepared for anything life can bring.

Having open discussions with our kids about these concepts is part of the reason why they work so well for us, and I'd encourage you to do the same. We're very transparent with our kids about our intentions. For example, we remind the Bigs regularly that it's our goal to make sure they become successful teenagers and in turn, successful adults, and we firmly believe that these principles will get them there. Of course, they laugh when they hear we're writing a book, because even though they know we were spies, we're just Dad and Christina to them. And when you're a teenager, what do your parents really know about anything, anyway? The journey isn't over, for us or for them, but we're confident they'll lean heavily on their security-awareness techniques and well-roundedness to help them to continue to succeed in life.

The journey for Ari and Gigi is far from over, and as we prepare to see the Bigs off to college over the next few years, we're looking forward to the many adventures we have in store with the Littles and the ways in which we'll continue to teach them these CIA techniques to prepare them for the world. Ryan and I often think how lucky Ari and Gigi are that they've had *both* of us from the time they were born. Not just one, but two former spies for parents, who have come together to create one very unique parenting approach to set them up for success in life. The Littles may not live in foreign lands like the Bigs did with Ryan when they were young, but we can't wait to take them to some of our favorite spots and show them how to travel like a spy. My passion for Africa carries on, and I look forward to returning there, not as an CIA officer, but as a mother excited to introduce her kids to the land that shaped the trajectory of her adult life. I've already begun preparing Ari and Gigi; in fact, we regularly take imaginary airplanes to Africa during playtime. It's no secret that I miss my time as an analyst at the CIA, but these days, I'm most excited about all the new and very different chapters in my life, most of which quite literally wouldn't be possible without my time at the Agency.

After a long day of playing outside with the kids, I had forgotten all about the spy shirt, until Ryan and I were getting into bed that night.

"You know, Ari and Gigi weren't even born yet when we were at the Agency," I pondered out loud. "It's like we had this whole other life before they even existed."

"Yeah, you're right. Will they even believe us?" he asked.

We both laughed. Sometimes we don't believe it ourselves.

ACKNOWLEDGMENTS

Thank you to Ryan for being my partner in life and in the writing of this book. Thank you for the countless late nights at the kitchen table hashing out these chapters, for hotel staycations so that I could write for extended periods away from the kids, and for always giving my writing a critical eye, even when I don't want to hear your changes. I'll always be in awe of your parenting abilities; I feel grateful that I get to do it alongside you every day. Thank you for loving our family so well and giving us so much of you, even when that often means there's very little left for yourself.

Thank you to Hannah, Hunter, and Lena for the grace you've given me as I've learned what it means to be your stepmom. Thank you for your endless love for Ari and Gigi; they may be the luckiest of all to have the three of you in their corner. And most of all, thank you for letting me share our stories.

Thank you to Ari and Gigi. I am so grateful that I get to be your mommy. You may not remember many of these times, but someday, when you're old enough to read these pages, I hope you can relive them and know how much you were loved by Daddy, the Bigs, and me.

Thank you to our literary agent, Howard Yoon, at Ross Yoon Agency. You saw something in our proposal and weren't afraid to take a chance on first-time authors, and for that, we'll always be grateful. You calmly and deftly guided us through a world that was new to us, all the while keeping us relaxed by reminding us to "trust the process." We're glad we did!

Thank you to the fantastic team at Putnam. There are few moments in someone's life when she knows she's exactly where she's supposed to be. I had one of these when I walked into your lobby in Manhattan and looked up at all the books you've published over many decades stacked along the walls. Indeed, it felt more natural and at home to me than the day I walked over the marble seal at CIA Headquarters for the first time. Thank you to our talented and gifted editor, Michelle Howry. Your ability to tease out the story you knew needed to be told from our proposal has been a game changer. Your extremely organized emails and track changes make this author's heart pitter-patter, and each and every careful edit from you has improved this manuscript. There are few people who can coin a phrase such as "busty, lusty man-eaters," and we're so glad you're one of them! Thank you for making this vision a reality for us. Thank you also to the following at Putnam: Ivan Held, president; Sally Kim, publisher; Ashley McClay, director of marketing; Alexis Welby, director of publicity; Ashley Di Dio, editorial assistant; Kristin del Rosario, interior designer; Kym Surridge, copy editor; Laura Rosenblum, senior counsel; and to Monica Cordova for her perfect cover design.

Thank you to our film agent, Jody Hotchkiss, for your stellar deal-making skills to bring this book to the screen. We're thankful to Howard for connecting us to you and that you enthusiastically chose to come onto this project. Onward!

Thank you to Ron Howard, Brian Grazer, and the entire team at Imagine Entertainment, especially Jillian Kugler, SVP, Imagine Television; and Anna Culp, EVP, Imagine Television. Jillian and Anna: thank you for connecting with our story and going above and beyond to get to know our family. In a world of pandemic Zoom meetings, you quite literally had us at "Hello" in a simple, old-fashioned phone call. Your passion for your work radiates through every form of communication, and we're so excited to be on this journey with you. We'll always save a spot for you to be the Biggest Bigs.

Thank you to my mom, who I'm more grateful for each and every day since becoming a mother myself. While I've learned a lot from Ryan's parenting, there's no one I've learned more from than you. Thank you for sacrificing so much of yourself to give to us kids and now your grandkids. Most days don't go by without a phone call with you, and usually, it's me blabbering on while you listen. Thank you for your unending support through every chapter of my life and for believing in me as a writer well before I landed a literary agent.

Thank you to my dad for always believing in me and bragging about my accomplishments to everyone he knows—from the days of rooting for me on the basketball court (even though I spent most of the game on the floor) to the day I got my offer from the CIA to when I became a published author. Your international travel inspired me to do the same, and I'm grateful to have inherited not just your dark hair, but your gregarious, life-of-the-party personality. Thank you for your love for me and for the family I've created with Ryan in the Pacific Northwest.

Thank you to my late brother, Michael. I wish more than anything that you were here to hold this book in your hands and share this joy with me. So much of this is because of you. You were my role model growing up and helped me choose my path of study. Your intellectual abilities were unrivaled, although I've certainly tried to keep up. I see you in Ari every day, and I'm grateful for that.

Thank you to Cathy, my supportive and loving sister. There are few people who know you throughout all your stages in life and love you just the same, and that's you for me. There's a love and mutual respect between us no matter what we choose to do, and I know how rare that is. Thank you for being the best auntie the kids could ask for.

Thank you to my stepfather, Dean. Thank you for being a guiding light for me in my formative college and postcollege years. I never sought out becoming a stepparent, and I'm sure you didn't either. It's a tricky role—I know that now—and it's one you have done with ease over the years, when I know we adult stepchildren didn't always make it easy on you. Thank you for loving my mom and our whole family with no expectations of anything in return.

Thank you to Papaw Green, who I grew up believing was an award-winning brain surgeon but later learned was a farmer, milkman, painter, and, of course, father and husband. Thank you for demonstrating what hard work looks like and for the life you and Mamaw began building for our family many years ago. You'll always be so much more than a brain surgeon to me.

Thank you to my in-laws, Ric and Sylvie, for your selfless love for Ryan, me, and the kids. Thank you for welcoming me into your family after Ryan's divorce and trusting me to help parent your grandkids and love them as my own children. From handling all the decorating at our wedding reception to helping us remodel our home, you're always willing to jump in when we need you. Thank you most of all for raising such an amazing man, whom I'm lucky to call my husband.

Thank you to Grandmama for your love and support in all of life's biggest and smallest moments. Your unending love for Papa is an example to all of us. The two of you created a beautiful, strong family, and I'm thankful to be a part of it.

Thank you to Jerry for teaching me how to write and believing in me before I believed in myself. I can confidently say that I wouldn't be where I am today without you taking me under your wing and helping me find my inner Stella. Those were the glory days, indeed. Thank you for editing my very first manuscript, which I'm sure you've recognized in some of these pages.

Thank you to our friend and photographer, Gabriel Van Wyhe. Your generosity and talent are unmatched, and we're grateful for your support. Who knew a chance encounter at the Bavarian Lodge would lead to all of this?

Thank you to the following friends and colleagues for your special input and support in bringing this book to fruition: Marissa Dever, Erick Amick, Henri, Alexa, Kent, Jennifer C., Nicole Steiner, Shannon Sherrill, Lauren Fosberry, Julie Morgan, Rachel Hoerman, Charise Apken, Kristen Kish, Nina Lindsey, Cameron "Steez" Masters, Suren Seron, Kami Vestman, and all the women of the Hive of Mama Be Strong.

Thank you to the following friends who provided insight into the publishing world: Karen Cleveland, Kristin Harmel, Sarah Carlson, Jenna Land Free, and Jenness Starks.

Thank you to the CIA PRB for your careful review of this manuscript to ensure we didn't inadvertently disclose classified information with what we've shared.

Last, thank you to our CIA colleagues. Thank you for your tireless work in the shadows to keep us all safe. Your failures are known, but your successes aren't, of which we know there are many. We're lucky to have worked among you, some of the most talented and extraordinary people we have ever met. Once you work at the CIA, nothing else holds a candle to it, especially the caliber of people. Keep fighting the good fight.

NOTES

Chapter 4

1 "Coronavirus Update: More People Growing 'Victory Gardens' for Food and Stress Relief," CBS New York video, 1:58, March 30, 2020, https://newyork.cbslocal.com/2020/03/30/coronavirus-update-more-people-growing-victory-gardens-for-food-and-stress-relief/amp/.

2 Mark Hatmaker, "A Conversation with Dr. John Huth Author of *The Lost Art of Finding Our Way*," *Indigenous Ability* (blog), November 20, 2017, http://indigenousability.blogspot.com/2017/11/a-conversation-with-dr-john-huth-author.html.

Chapter 5

1 Lee Glendinning, "9/11 Survivors Put Off Evacuation to Shut Down Computers, Study Finds," *Guardian*, September 9, 2008, https://www.theguardian.com/world/2008/sep/09/september11.usa.

2 Sean Lavery, "The Sinking of the M.V. Sewol and the Confusion of Disasters," *New Yorker*, April 9, 2019.

Chapter 9

1 Jack Davis, "Improving CIA Analytic Performance: Analysts and the Policymaking Process," Sherman Kent Center for Intelligence Analysis, https://www.cia.gov/library/kent-center-occasional-papers/pdf/OPNo2.pdf.
2 Frank Newport, "The New Era of Communication Among Americans," Gallup, November 10, 2014, https://news.gallup.com/poll/179288/new-era-communication-americans.aspx.
3 Neil Howe, "Why Millennials Are Texting More and Talking Less," *Forbes*, July 15, 2015, https://www.forbes.com/sites/neilhowe/2015/07/15/why-millennials-are-texting-more-and-talking-less/#612cf08d5975.
4 Howe, "Why Millennials Are Texting More and Talking Less."

Chapter 11

1 Bruce Riedel, "The Remarkable Case of the Triple Agent and the Bombing in Khost, Afghanistan," Brookings, December 6, 2019, https://www.brookings.edu/blog/order-from-chaos/2019/12/06/the-remarkable-case-of-the-triple-agent-and-the-bombing-in-khost-afghanistan/.
2 Jeff Thompson, "Is Nonverbal Communication a Numbers Game?" *Psychology Today*, September 30, 2011, https://www.psychologytoday.com/us/blog/beyond-words/201109/is-nonverbal-communication-numbers-game.

Chapter 12

1 Deanna Paul, "A Teen Traded Naked Selfies with Girls His Age. A Court Is Making Him Register as a Sex Offender," *Washington Post*, June 27, 2019, https://www.washingtonpost.com/nation/2019/06/27/teen-traded-naked-selfies-with-girls-his-age-court-is-making-him-register-sex-offender/.
2 "Teens Say the Tracking App Life360 Is Ruining Their Summer," *ABC News* video, 3:14, July 17, 2019, https://abcnews.go.com/GMA/Family/video/teens-tracking-app-life360-ruining-summer-64385463.
3 Sarah O'Brien, "Employers Check Your Social Media Before Hiring. Many Then Find Reasons Not to Offer You a Job," *CNBC*, August 10, 2018, https://www.cnbc.com/2018/08/10/digital-dirt-may-nix-that-job-you-were-counting-on-getting.html.
4 O'Brien, "Employers Check Your Social Media."

5 "Indicators of School Crime and Safety—Indicator 10: Bullying at School and Electronic Bullying," National Center for Education Statistics, updated April 2019, https://nces.ed.gov/programs/crimeindicators/ind_10.asp.

Chapter 13

1 Megan Leonhardt, "1 in 5 Millennials with Debt Expect to Die Without Ever Paying It Off," *CNBC*, January 9, 2019, https://www.cnbc.com/2019/01/08/1-in-5-millennials-with-debt-expect-to-die-without-ever-paying-it-off.html.

INDEX

ABOUT THE AUTHORS

Christina and Ryan Hillsberg are former spies with more than twenty years of experience working at the Central Intelligence Agency before transitioning to the private sector. They live near Seattle, Washington, with their five children and two Rhodesian ridgebacks.

Christina

While at the CIA, Christina spent the majority of her career working on and traveling to Africa as one of the intelligence community's few Swahili and Zulu linguists. As an analyst in the Directorate of Intelligence, she wrote analytic assessments on topics such as political unrest, insurgencies, and authoritarian regimes for the president, his cabinet, and other senior-level policymakers. She spent the final portion of her time at the Agency working alongside her colleagues in the Directorate of Operations, where she learned firsthand how to clandestinely collect intelligence in the field. She is the recipient of multiple CIA Exceptional Performance Awards. After leaving the CIA, Christina worked in information security at Amazon, where she created and developed the company's first insider threat program, created a new global framework to analyze cyber risks, and established new processes to utilize intelligence tradecraft to analyze information security threats. She then transitioned to Amazon public relations, where she incorporated security awareness techniques into PR guidance for employees to ensure confidentiality of drones and test sites for Amazon Prime Air, the company's drone delivery program. In 2017, she began a new chapter as a stay-at-home mom and started her own fitness company.

Ryan

Fluent in French, Danish, and Portuguese, Ryan spent his CIA career recruiting spies and stealing secrets in Europe and around the world. As an operations officer, he was tasked with running foreign intelligence operations and collecting strategic intelligence on issues such as counterterrorism, counterproliferation, nuclear security, political instability, covert action, and other state secrets. Ryan received several CIA Exceptional Performance Awards and was the CIA's top regional intelligence producer during two separate CIA tours overseas. After leaving the CIA, he worked for the Pacific Northwest National Laboratory (PNNL), a Department of Energy (DOE) Office of Science laboratory focused on national security. As a senior technical adviser, Ryan's primary responsibility was business development between the laboratory and the intelligence community. During that time, he also ran an emerging objective on insider threat, managed the DOE polygraph program, and helped PNNL's Seattle strategy in linking the private sector with government agencies in the intelligence community.

After PNNL, Ryan joined Amazon, where he led worldwide security for Amazon Prime Air and was responsible for the security of worldwide facilities, personnel, and intellectual property. In addition, he was the Global Security Operations representative for Amazon's enterprise-wide insider threat program. He is the current director of corporate security at Seagen, a global biotechnology company.